More recipes from the backs of boxes, bottles, cans and jars

Books by Ceil Dyer:

The After-Work Entertaining Cookbook
Carter Family Favorites Cookbook
The Chopped, Minced and Ground Meat Cookbook
Coffee Cookery
The Eat to Lose Cookbook
Freezer to Oven to Table
Plan-Ahead Cookbook
Wok Cookery
Best Recipes from the Backs of Boxes, Bottles,
    Cans and Jars

More recipes from the backs of boxes, bottles, cans and jars

by Ceil Dyer

McGraw-Hill Book Company

New York   St. Louis   San Francisco
Toronto   Düsseldorf   Mexico

1 2 3 4 5 6 7 8 9 FG FG 9 8 7 6 5 4 3 2 1

LIBRARY OF CONGRESS CATALOGING IN PUBLICATION DATA

Dyer, Ceil.
More recipes from the backs of boxes, bottles, cans & jars.
Includes index.
1. Cookery. I. Title.
TX715.D9777   641.5   81-1602
ISBN 0-07-018554-9   AACR2
ISBN 0-07-018555-7 (pbk.)

Contents

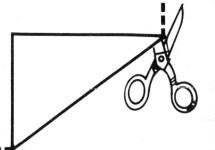

We wish to thank the following for permission to use these recipes:

Thomas J. Lipton, Inc.
Del Monte Corporation
San Giorgio Macaroni, Inc.
Armour and Company
Castle & Cooke Foods
    Division of Castle & Cooke, Inc.
Hunt-Wesson Kitchens
The Procter & Gamble Company
Best Foods, A Division of CPC
    INTERNATIONAL, INC.
William J. Underwood Company
Kikkoman International, Inc.
Welch Foods, Inc.
Pepperidge Farm
Lea & Perrins, Inc.
Campbell Soup Company
Kraft, Inc.
Libby, McNeill & Libby, Inc.
C. F. Mueller Company
The R. T. French Company
Wish-Bone

Elam's
Hershey Foods Corp.
American Pop Corn Company
    (JOLLY TIME Popcorn)
Riviana Foods, Inc.
Nabisco, Inc.
Oscar Mayer & Co.
Gerber Products Company
Green Giant Company
Ralston Purina Company
Pet, Inc.
Frito-Lay, Inc. (DORITOS/FRITOS)
Pillsbury BAKE-OFF®
McIlhenny Company
Sun-Land Marketing
General Mills, Inc. (Betty Crocker)
General Foods Corp.
Uncle Ben's, Inc.
California Almond Growers
    Exchange

Introduction

"Come with me down Memory Lane." That's what one reader said about our first collection of *Best Recipes from the Backs of Boxes, Bottles, Cans and Jars*. She recalled the foods she had loved as a child—and still does. Well, I guess many of us get nostalgic about favorite recipes we loved and somehow lost—recipes clipped, saved, and then misplaced.

Now, in response to your enthusiasm for our first book, here is its companion volume, filled to the last page with the all-American, all-time best recipes, from deep-fried crispy croquettes (how I remember these—we always had them with creamed peas!) to real chocolaty chocolate fudge. Here are the appetizers, soups, main dishes, salads and sandwiches, breads and cakes, cookies and candies you will remember and can now enjoy again.

Occasionally, we have included some brand-new dishes we feel are destined to become the favorites of tomorrow. (Just try the unbelievable lasagne or the Bisquick fresh vegetable appetizers!)

Each and every recipe in every chapter in this book is so accurate, so easy to follow, you simply can't miss; and well they should be, for each one is from the test kitchens of our very best food producers. I just wish I could be as free to experiment as the home economists of our food producers. If they have an inspiration, they can throw caution to the winds and go full steam ahead. If the results are not to their liking, never mind, throw it out and try again. Well, friends, not so in my kitchen, those two sticks of butter I used in my last culinary experiment still haunt me, the price of butter being what it is. So it's extra nice—and far less expensive—to have all these wonderful dishes perfected by someone else!

As in our first book each recipe has been tested and retested by these experts. You can prepare every one with confidence and serve them with pride for these are the foods America loves; our own unique cuisine, a blend, like our country itself, of many cultures, the heritage of good cooks from all over the world.

All are easy to prepare, every ingredient is readily available and each is truly a classic.

1.

Main Course Dishes: Beef, Pork, Chicken, Fish, Pasta and Main Dish Pies

I have a friend to whom "main course" means only one thing—red meat. "Now I like a meal to *mean* something," he says. "Anyone who sits a dinner plate down in front of me without red meat on it is going to get it right back." By meat he generally means beef, and who doesn't like a juicy, flavorful steak? But even if steak were not so expensive, who wouldn't tire of it night after night? That's why I love the beef recipes I've collected for this book: there are all manner of recipes for inexpensive cuts of beef to prepare with ease and serve with pleasure. And that's not all; the beef recipes are followed by some mighty tasty ideas for pork, even for humble franks that taste so good the avid steak lover will compromise "just this once."

Now my friend said he would send the plate back if it did not include red meat, but I doubt he would return a platter of just perfect fried chicken or chicken and wild rice supreme. And it is hardly likely anyone would send back untasted a plate of charcoal-grilled Sunshine chicken. Well hardly! As a matter of fact, all of the recipes in our main-dish chapter are (like the rest of the book) "asked for" favorites; every one has taken encores from the fans. Proof enough that they are unsurpassed for just plain deliciousness.

In addition to beef, pork and chicken recipes, there are fish specialties ranging from crispy fish 'n' chips to a delicate Flounder au Gratin, special enough for a dinner party.

I challenge anyone to send any of them back to the kitchen.

As for pasta, no self-respecting cookbook would go to press without a portfolio of recipes for America's favorite ethnic food. And what pasta recipes! Easier than ever, kinder than a rich uncle to the budget, and as popular as peanuts at the circus. They include some totally new ways to prepare your favorites and I know you'll love them. Last, but not least, a few delicate quiches and main-course pies, lovely stars for a luncheon party and a sophisticated choice for festive supper.

Western Pot Roast

This pot roast is standard fare when there are hungry men around. Lea & Perrins perfected the recipe and it's been a favorite for over a decade.

3 lbs. beef brisket or boneless round or chuck roast	¼ cup Lea & Perrins Worcestershire Sauce
1 cup chopped onion	2 Tbs. brown sugar
1 cup catsup	2 Tbs. cider vinegar
	2 tsps. salt

In heavy pot brown on all sides beef brisket or boneless round or chuck roast in oil. Add chopped onion; cook until golden. Combine catsup, Lea & Perrins Worcestershire Sauce, brown sugar, cider vinegar and salt; pour over meat. Simmer, covered, until meat is tender, about 3 hours. Serve sliced with sauce along with onions, carrots and potato chunks if desired. Serves 8.

Marinated Steak Italiano

You know this recipe but had just forgotten? Well remember and enjoy. It's Wish-Bone's contribution to the pleasures of charcoal cookery.

2½- to 3-lb. London broil or chuck steak
  ½ cup Wish-Bone Italian Dressing

In large baking dish, place meat and cover with Wish-Bone Italian Dressing. Marinate, turning occasionally, about 3 hours. Broil steak, preferably over charcoal, turning once. Makes about 6 servings.

Variation: Add ¼ cup soy sauce and ¼ cup brown sugar to Wish-Bone® Italian Dressing before marinating.

Onion Chuck Steak

From Lipton comes one of the best tasting, easy, "bake-in-foil" dishes I've ever tasted. Serve it with baked potatoes and broiled tomato slices for a cooked all-in-the oven meal.

1½ lb. boneless chuck steak
  2 envelopes Lipton Onion Cup-a-Soup
  1 2½-oz. jar sliced mushrooms, drained

Preheat oven to 375°F. Place meat on foil in shallow baking pan. Sprinkle both sides with Lipton Onion Cup-a-Soup; top with mushrooms. Wrap loosely, sealing airtight with double fold; bake 1 hour. Makes about 4 servings.

Swiss Steak

Another Campbell soup label recipe that remains consistently in favor. Not just because it's easy, they told me at the

Campbell Test Kitchens, but because this particular combination of steak and sauce happens to be especially good.

1½ lb. round steak
1 Tbs. vegetable shortening
½ cup chopped canned tomatoes
¼ cup chopped onion
¼ cup water
Dash pepper

Pound steak; cut into serving-size pieces. In heavy skillet, brown steak in shortening; pour off fat. Add remaining ingredients. Cover; simmer 1½ hours or until done. Stir often. Makes 4–6 servings.

Kikkoman Chuck Steak Teriyaki

An original American-Oriental recipe from Kikkoman. Inexpensive chuck steak is basted with a thick tomato-teri sauce and grilled to juicy, tender perfection.

2½ lb. chuck steak (about 1½ inches thick)
Meat tenderizer
⅔ cup Kikkoman Teriyaki Sauce
1 6-oz. can tomato paste
¼ cup salad oil

Prepare meat with a meat tenderizer according to label directions. Combine remaining 3 ingredients; brush over meat. Place on grill 3–4 inches from hot coals. Cook about 15 minutes. Turn steak over and brush with additional sauce. Cook to desired degree of doneness. Heat remaining sauce and serve with steak. Makes 4 servings.

New England Boiled Dinner

New Englanders know what to put on the table on a frosty night: it's this classic boiled dinner; and you know something, they are so right. Campbell's makes it easy for you to make it perfect. Warm gingerbread with whipped cream for dessert, anyone?

3 lb. boneless beef round rump roast
2 tsps. shortening
2 10¾-oz. cans Campbell's Onion Soup
1 tsp. prepared horseradish
1 medium bay leaf
1 medium clove garlic, minced
6 medium carrots (about 1 lb.) peeled & cut in 2-inch pieces

1 lb. rutabagas, peeled & sliced ¼-inch thick
8 whole potatoes (about 1 lb.), peeled
1 medium head cabbage (about 2 lbs.) cut in 6 wedges
½ cup water
¼ cup flour

In large heavy pan, brown meat in shortening; pour off fat. Add soup, horseradish, bay leaf, and garlic. Cover; cook over low heat 2 hours. Add carrots and rutabagas. Cook 30 minutes. Stir occasionally. Add potatoes; place cabbage on top. Cook 30 minutes more or until done. Remove meat and vegetables to serving platter; keep warm. Meanwhile, blend water into flour until smooth; stir into sauce. Cook, stirring until thickened. Makes 6 servings.

Salisbury Steak

The 1930's: President-elect Roosevelt was soon to be in the White House, "prosperity was just around the corner" and "things were sure to get better," but hourly wages were still only 44¢. In Depression days ingenious cooks believed "there

just had to be another way to cook hamburger." There was: Salisbury steak. You may not believe it, but some people, including me, like it better than porterhouse. You may too when you try this version from the French Company.

1 egg
½ cup dry bread crumbs
½ cup tomato juice
1 Tbs. French's Minced Onions
1 lb. ground beef
1 envelope French's Mushroom Gravy Mix
1 cup water

Combine egg, bread crumbs, tomato juice and onions; add ground beef. Shape into oblong patties, brown in skillet. Add gravy mix and water, stirring until smooth. Cover and simmer 10 minutes. Makes 4 servings.

Beef Burgundy with Rice

An American adaptation of a French classic from the Uncle Ben's® rice box that's just as great tasting as it is easy to prepare.

5 medium onions, thinly sliced
2 Tbs. bacon drippings or shortening
2 lbs. boneless beef chuck, cut into 1½-inch
  cubes
2 Tbs. flour
  Salt, pepper, thyme, marjoram to taste
½ cup beef bouillon
1 cup dry red wine
½ pound fresh mushrooms, sliced
4 cups hot cooked Uncle Ben's ® Converted
  Brand Rice

In heavy skillet, cook onions in bacon drippings until brown. Remove onions and set aside. Add more bacon drippings to skillet if necessary. Add beef cubes to drippings and brown well on all sides. Sprinkle beef with flour and seasonings. Stir in bouillon and wine. Cover and simmer very slowly for 2½–3 hours, or until meat is tender. If necessary, add more bouillon and red wine (1 part bouillon to 2 parts wine) to keep the meat barely covered with the liquid. Return onions to pan and add mushrooms. Cook 30 minutes longer, adding more liquid if necessary. Adjust seasonings to taste. Serve over hot cooked rice.

Dutch Meat Loaf

One of the most requested label recipes from Hunt's Tomato Sauce. The brown sugar tomato sauce topping makes it especially good.

1½ lbs. lean ground beef
 1 cup fresh bread crumbs
 1 medium onion, chopped
 1 8-oz. can Hunt's Tomato Sauce
 1 egg
1½ tsps. salt
 ¼ tsp. pepper
 ¾ cup water
 2 Tbs. brown sugar, packed
 2 Tbs. prepared mustard
 1 Tbs. vinegar

In medium bowl, lightly mix beef, bread crumbs, onion, ½ can Hunt's Tomato Sauce, egg, salt and pepper. Shape into loaf in shallow baking pan. Combine remaining Hunt's Sauce with rest of ingredients; pour over loaf. Bake at 350°F. 1¼ hours. Baste loaf several times. Makes 5–6 servings.

Rodeo Hash

This quick cooking, one-skillet supper dish has gained in popularity over the years. It's one of the best from Campbell's back-of-the-label recipes.

1 lb. ground beef
3 cups diced raw potatoes
1 cup sliced celery
2 T. shortening
1 can Campbell's Golden
  Mushroom Soup

½ cup water
¼ cup chili sauce
½ tsp. salt
  Generous dash pepper

In skillet, brown beef in shortening with potatoes and celery; stir to separate meat. Pour off fat. Add remaining ingredients. Cover; simmer 10 minutes. Stir often. Makes 4½ cups.

Chili Beef and Beans

A chili con carne dish that's ready in 15 minutes on top of the stove. It's one of the ever popular "adaptable" recipes developed by the home economists at Campbell's test kitchen. I garnish this dish with avocado slices, minced green onion and grated Monterey Jack cheese. No doubt, you'll have your own ideas.

1 lb. ground beef
1 cup chopped onion
1 large clove garlic, minced
2 tsps. chili power
2 16-oz. cans Campbell's Pork and Beans in
  Tomato Sauce
1 10-oz. can tomatoes and green chilies

In large saucepan, brown beef and cook onion, combined with garlic and chili powder, until tender (use shortening if necessary); stir to separate meat. Add remaining ingredients. Bring to boil; reduce heat. Simmer 10 minutes; stir occasionally. Makes about 6½ cups, 6 servings.

Veal Goulash

Originally a Hungarian dish, this goulash is so good it has become an international favorite. Easy and economical, it's a great choice for a buffet supper. The recipe is from the Planters Peanut Oil cookbook.

2 lbs. veal cubes
1 Tbs. paprika
¼ cup Planters Peanut Oil
1¼ cups chopped onions
2 medium tomatoes, peeled and wedged
1 8-oz. can tomato sauce
2 tsps. salt
Hot cooked noodles

Dredge veal with paprika, set aside. Heat Planters Peanut Oil in Dutch oven. Add chopped onions and sauté until lightly browned; remove onions using slotted spoon and set aside. Brown dredged veal on all sides. Return onions to Dutch oven. Stir in tomatoes, tomato sauce and salt. Simmer gently, uncovered, about 1 hour, or until veal is tender. Serve over noodles. Makes about 6 servings.

Meatballs with Spaghetti

No collection of American favorites would be complete without this Italian-style dish. Hunt's has perfected the recipe for the label of their Tomato Paste can.

2 eggs, beaten
2 6-oz. or 1 12-oz. can
   Hunt's Tomato Paste
¼ cup minced onion
¼ cup grated Parmesan
   cheese
2 Tbs. minced parsley
1 clove garlic,
   minced
2 tsp. Salt

1 lb. ground beef
¾ cup soft bread crumbs
3 Tbs. pure vegetable oil
2½ cups hot water
1½ tsps. sugar
1 tsp. basil
1 tsp. oregano
¼ tsp. pepper
1 lb. spaghetti, cooked
   and drained

In a bowl, mix together eggs, 1 Tbs. Hunt's Tomato Paste, onion, cheese, parsley, garlic and 1 tsp. salt. Add beef and bread crumbs; mix thoroughly. Form into 20 balls, about 1 inch in diameter. Lightly brown in a Dutch oven on all sides in hot oil; drain fat. Blend remaining Hunt's Tomato Paste with hot water, sugar, basil, oregano, 1 tsp. salt and the pepper in a bowl. Pour over meatballs. Cover; simmer 10 minutes. Uncover; simmer 10 minutes longer. Serve over spaghetti. Makes 6 servings.

Golden Glaze Ham

Armour tells me this is a Midwest farm recipe and I can believe it. Only a good farm cook would dream up using a jar of apple jelly to glaze a ham and is it delicious!

1 5-lb. Armour Golden Star Ham
1 10-oz. jar apple jelly
1 tsp. lemon juice
½ tsp. cinnamon
    Dash of nutmeg

Heat oven to 325°F. Score surface of ham. Heat ham according to label instructions. Combine remaining ingredients in small saucepan. Heat, stirring occasionally, until jelly melts. Spoon glaze over ham during last 30 minutes of heating time.

Pork Chops Parisienne

An old-world recipe to prepare in new-world record time. I found it, of all places, on a package of Del Monte dried pitted prunes. I think you'll be glad I did.

4 1-inch center cut pork chops
1 cup dry white wine
12 Del Monte Pitted Prunes
1 cup heavy whipping cream
1 Tbs. red currant jelly

In skillet, brown pork chops. Add ¼ cup wine and simmer, covered, 25 minutes. Place Del Monte prunes and ¾ cup wine in oven-proof dish; heat in 300°F. oven for 20 minutes. Remove pork chops to heated platter. To skillet add whipping cream and currant jelly; cook quickly over high heat, stirring constantly, until sauce is thick and shiny. Pour over pork chops. Garnish with baked prunes in wine.

Pork Chops 'n' Vegetables

This is an old favorite from Lea & Perrins advertising. It's a soul-satisfying dish that needs only some good crusty bread and a crisp salad to round out the meal. Reheatable too for make-ahead cooks.

2 Tbs. oil
6 pork loin chops, ½-inch thick
1 green pepper, cut into strips
2 Tbs. flour
1 10½-oz. can condensed onion soup
2 Tbs. Lea & Perrins Worcestershire Sauce
1 tsp. garlic powder
1 tsp. salt
2 medium tomatoes, cut in wedges

In large skillet heat oil. Add chops, 3 at a time; brown well on both sides; remove and set aside. Add green pepper; sauté for 3 minutes; remove and set aside. Stir in flour; cook and stir for 1 minute. Blend in next 4 ingredients. Bring to boiling point. Return chops to skillet; spoon sauce over chops. Cover and simmer until chops are tender, about 1 hour. Stir in tomatoes and sautéed green pepper. Cover and simmer 5 minutes longer. Serves 6.

Sweet and Sour Pork Skillet

If you like pork, you'll love this recipe. It's been an all-time favorite since 1957 when it first appeared on the back of the Uncle Ben's ® Converted Brand Rice package.

1 lb. boneless pork, cut in
  ¾-inch cubes
1 13½-oz. can pineapple
  tidbits
¼ cup vinegar
1½ tsps. salt
½ tsp. garlic salt

2 Tbs. sugar
1 cup Uncle Ben's®
  Converted Brand Rice
1 green pepper, cut into
  small squares
1 tomato, cut into thin
  wedges

Brown pork in cooking oil in 10-inch skillet; drain. Drain
pineapple tidbits, reserving liquid. Add water to liquid to
make 2½ cups. Add liquid, vinegar, salt, garlic salt and
sugar to pork; stir. Bring to boil. Reduce heat, cover and
cook over low heat 20 minutes. Remove cover, stir in rice.
Cover and continue cooking about 25 minutes or until
liquid is absorbed and pork is tender. Stir in pineapple
tidbits, green pepper and tomato wedges. Heat through.
Makes 4–6 servings.

Variations: Nice to add sliced water chestnuts or bam-
boo shoots at end of cooking, or substitute cubed ham or
cubed uncooked chicken for pork.

Braised Ginger Pork

**Nobody seems to have a better knack for Chinese dishes than
the Planters Peanut Oil cooks. After all Peanut Oil *is* the
traditional cooking oil of China.**

2 lbs. lean 1-inch pork cubes
  Flour
3 Tbs. Planters Peanut Oil
⅓ cup chicken broth
⅓ cup soy sauce
2 Tbs. sherry
¼ cup chopped green or yellow onion
1 small clove garlic, crushed or minced

1 Tbs. sugar
1 tsp. ground ginger
  Dash pepper
  Hot cooked rice

Dredge meat in flour. Heat Planters Peanut Oil in Dutch oven or large skillet. Add half of meat and brown quickly; remove meat and set aside. Brown remaining meat; remove and set aside. Pour off excess oil from pan. Combine chicken broth, soy sauce and sherry. Add onion, garlic, sugar, ginger and pepper. Place in cooking pan along with meat. Simmer, covered, for 15 minutes, or until meat is tender. Serve over rice. Makes about 6 servings.

Speedy Baked Beans with Wieners

The Oscar Mayer Company tells me that this quick-cooking baked beans recipe has been a consumer favorite ever since it first appeared on their bacon package a decade ago.

1 8-oz. package Oscar Mayer Bacon
3 1-lb. cans baked beans
½ cup chopped onion
¼ cup firmly packed brown sugar
1 Tbs. molasses
2 tsps. Worcestershire sauce
½ tsp. dry mustard
1 1-lb. package Oscar Mayer Wieners cut up

Cut bacon into 1-inch pieces; cook in skillet until crisp; add remaining ingredients. Simmer, covered, for 15 minutes. Makes 6 servings.

Country Fried Chicken

As American as the Fourth of July—and just right for a picnic. This country fried chicken has been a "most requested favorite" ever since it was first developed especially for the back label of the Crisco shortening can.

1 2½- to 3-lb. frying
chicken, cut-up or use
chicken pieces
Crisco Shortening
½ cup milk
1 egg
1 cup flour

2 tsps. garlic salt
2 tsps. MSG
1 tsp. paprika
¼ tsp. poultry seasoning
1 tsp. black pepper

Blend milk and egg. Combine flour and seasonings in plastic or paper bag. Shake chicken in seasoned flour. Dip chicken pieces in milk/egg mixture. Shake chicken a *second* time in seasoning mixture to coat thoroughly and evenly.

To Pan Fry: Melt Crisco in skillet to about ½- to 1-inch deep and heat to 365°F. Brown chicken on all sides. Reduce heat (275°F.) and continue cooking until chicken is tender, about 30–40 minutes. Do not cover. Turn chicken several times during cooking. Drain on paper towels.

To Deep Fry: Prepare as above and cook in deep Crisco heated to 365°F. for 15–18 minutes. Drain on paper towels. Makes about 4 servings.

Variation: For extra-spicy chicken: Increase poultry seasoning to ½ tsp. and black pepper to 2 tsps.

Oven-Fried Chicken

From the Betty Crocker Kitchens a sure-fire way to crispy, flavorful oven-fried chicken plus four interesting variations. An asked-for recipe for years and it's not surprising!

1 Tbs. margarine or butter
⅔ cup Bisquick® Baking Mix
1½ tsps. paprika
1¼ tsps. salt
¼ tsp. pepper
2½- to 3½-lb. broiler-fryer chicken, cut up

Heat oven to 425°F. Heat margarine in rectangular pan, 13 × 9 × 2 inches, until melted. Mix baking mix, paprika, salt and pepper; coat chicken. Place chicken, skin side down, in pan. Bake uncovered 35 minutes. Turn; bake until done, about 15 minutes longer. Makes 6 servings.

Variations:

Italian Coating: Add 1 Tbs. Italian seasoning and ½ tsp. garlic powder.

Mexican Coating: Decrease baking mix to ½ cup. Add 2 Tbs. cornmeal and 1 to 2 Tbs. chili powder.

Parmesan Coating: Decrease baking mix to ⅓ cup and salt to 1 tsp. Add ½ cup grated Parmesan cheese.

Sesame-Herb Coating: Decrease salt to 1 tsp. Add 2 Tbs. sesame seed and 2 tsps. each dried thyme leaves, ground sage and parsley flakes.

Zesty Orange Barbecued Chicken

Now when was it someone started using orange juice concentrate as a marinade? I don't remember, but those clever Kikkoman cooks give us an up-to-date version that combines it with Kikkoman Teriyaki Sauce for sensational results.

1 6-oz. can frozen orange juice concentrate,
    thawed
¼ cup Kikkoman Teriyaki Sauce
1 Tbs. instant minced onion
1 tsp. parsley flakes
½ tsp. garlic powder
¼ tsp. black pepper
8– 10 pieces frying chicken

Combine all ingredients, except chicken; let stand 10 minutes. Place chicken and sauce in large plastic bag; press air out and close securely. Refrigerate 8 hours or overnight, turning over occasionally. Remove chicken; reserve marinade. Place on grill 6–8 inches from hot coals. Cook about 20 minutes on each side; baste with reserved marinade during last 15 minutes of cooking time. Makes 6–8 servings.

Chicken Continental

This richly European-flavored entrée appeared recently in national magazines and has won hundreds of fans— including one woman who found herself in a dilemma when the recipe she clipped was lost forever behind her gigantic stove. But the story ended happily. When her letter reached the ever-obliging folks at Kikkoman, a specially typed replica was quickly sent to her.

3 lbs. frying chicken pieces
¼ cup flour (about)
2 Tbs. salad oil
1 4-oz. can sliced mushrooms
1 16-oz. can tomatoes, chopped
⅓ cup Kikkoman Soy Sauce
1 clove garlic, minced
1 medium onion, sliced
¼ cup sliced pitted black olives (optional)
3 cups hot cooked rice (cooked according to
   package directions)

Coat chicken pieces thoroughly with flour; brown slowly in hot oil. Meanwhile, drain mushrooms, reserving liquid. Combine mushroom liquid with tomatoes, soy sauce and garlic. Add to chicken with onion and stir to combine. Cover and simmer 45 minutes, or until chicken is tender. Stir in mushrooms and olives; bring to boil. Serve over fluffy rice. Pass additional soy sauce, if desired. Makes 4–6 servings.

Sunshine Chicken

A truly unusual and delicious recipe for a party cookout from the R. T. French Company.

¼ cup French's Prepared Mustard
¼ cup pineapple juice
1 Tbs. brown sugar
8 slices lean bacon
2 whole chicken breasts, split, boned, skinned and sliced in half crosswise, making 8 pieces in all.

In small mixing bowl, combine mustard, pineapple juice, and brown sugar, mixing until sugar is dissolved. Wrap each chicken piece with bacon, fastening with wooden picks. Brush mustard sauce over chicken and bacon. Grill over hot coals about 10 minutes, turning frequently and brushing with additional mustard sauce. Remove wooden picks. To serve, spoon remaining sauce over chicken. Makes 4 servings.

Pizza Chicken Italiano

Here's a rich Italian treatment for chicken devised by Del Monte for their "no taste like home" series of recipes.

2 whole chicken breasts (split, boned, skinned)
1 15-oz. can Del Monte Tomato Sauce
1½ tsp. oregano
1 tsp. chopped parsley
½ tsp. each garlic salt, onion powder and sugar
1 2¼-oz. can sliced ripe olives, drained
4 slices Mozzarella cheese

Place chicken in 2-quart baking dish. Combine tomato sauce, oregano, chopped parsley, garlic salt, onion powder and sugar. Pour over chicken, cover, and bake at 425°F. for 15 minutes. Top with olives and Mozzarella cheese and continue to bake, uncovered, for 10 minutes. Designed for oven-to-table service. Serves 4.

Wild Rice—Chicken Supreme

This is the recipe that convinced literally a million Americans that Uncle Ben's® Long Grain and Wild Rice was indeed worth the price.

1 6-oz. package Uncle Ben's® Long Grain and Wild Rice
¼ cup butter or margarine
⅓ cup chopped onion
⅓ cup flour
1 tsp. salt
Dash black pepper

1 cup half & half
1 cup chicken broth
2 cups cubed cooked chicken
⅓ cup chopped pimiento
⅓ cup chopped parsley
¼ cup chopped almonds

Prepare contents of rice and seasoning packets according to package directions. Meanwhile, melt butter in large saucepan. Add onion and cook over low heat until tender. Stir in flour, salt and pepper. Gradually stir in half & half and chicken broth. Cook, stirring constantly, until thickened. Stir in chicken, pimiento, parsley, almonds and cooked rice. Place in 2-quart casserole. Bake, uncovered, in 425°F. oven for 30 minutes. Makes 6–8 servings.

Savory Crescent Chicken Squares

**A $25,000 Grand Prize Winner at the 25th Pillsbury Bake-Off®
Contest in 1974, and it is good! Just about everybody wants
this recipe, so here it is. I like to serve it with a cream sauce
and tiny green peas.**

1 3-oz. package cream cheese, softened
3 Tbs. margarine or butter, melted
2 cups cubed cooked chicken or two 5-oz. cans
   boned chicken
¼ tsp. salt
⅛ tsp. pepper
2 Tbs. milk
1 Tbs. chopped chives or onion
1 Tbs. chopped pimiento, if desired
1 8-oz. can Pillsbury Refrigerated Quick
   Crescent Dinner Rolls
¾ cup seasoned croutons, crushed

Heat oven to 350°F. In medium bowl, blend cream cheese and 2 Tbs. of the margarine until smooth. Add next 6 ingredients; mix well. Separate dough into 4 rectangles; firmly press perforations around edges together to seal. Spoon ½ cup meat mixture onto center of each rectangle. Pull 4 corners of dough to top center of chicken mixture, twist slightly and seal edges. Place on ungreased cookie sheet. Brush tops with reserved 1 Tbs. margarine; sprinkle with crouton crumbs. Bake at 350°F. for 20–25 minutes or until golden brown. Serves 4.

Pineapple Chicken in Patty Shells

When we wanted to impress anybody back in Shreveport, Louisiana, we served creamed chicken in patty shells. Now Pepperidge Farm gives this elegant new version of an old favorite.

    1 package Pepperidge Farm Patty Shells
    ½ cup chopped onion
    2 Tbs. butter or margarine
    1 cup orange juice
    ¼ cup brown sugar
    1 8-oz. can undrained crushed pineapple
    ¼ tsp. ground cinnamon
    1½ Tbs. cornstarch
    2 cups cubed cooked chicken
    1 package frozen pea pods
    ¼ cup toasted slivered almonds

Prepare patty shells according to package directions. Meanwhile, in a saucepan, cook onion in butter until tender. Add orange juice, brown sugar, pineapple, cinnamon and cornstarch. Cook, stirring, over medium heat until thickened and smooth. Add chicken and pea pods and heat. Spoon into patty shells. Garnish with almonds. Makes 6 servings.

Country Cornish Hens

Sausage stuffing—as traditional as pumpkin pie in the heartland of America—now goes elegant with sherry-basted Rock Cornish hens. A special favorite from Parkay's test kitchens.

½ lb. bulk pork sausage
2 cups bread cubes, toasted
1 cup chopped, peeled apples
½ cup celery slices
⅓ cup raisins
⅓ cup chopped onion
¾ cup Parkay Margarine, melted

⅓ cup sherry
¼ tsp. sage
¼ tsp. salt
Dash of pepper
6 1- to 1½-lb. Rock Cornish hens

Brown meat; drain. Add bread, apples, celery, raisins, onion, ¼ cup margarine, 2 Tbs. sherry and seasonings; mix well. Lightly stuff hens with dressing mixture; close openings with skewers. Bake at 400°F. 1 hour or until tender, basting occasionally with combined remaining margarine and sherry. Garnish with celery leaves, if desired. Makes 6 servings.

Stuffed Turkey

No self-respecting Southerner would dream of using anything but corn bread stuffing for the holiday bird but now Campbell's has perfected a new variation on the traditional version that even a Yankee would love.

6 slices bacon
1 cup celery, sliced
½ cup chopped onion
1 8½-oz. package herb-seasoned stuffing mix
2 cups coarse cornbread crumbs
1 10½-oz. can Campbell's Condensed Chicken Broth

1 egg, slightly beaten
10-pound turkey
1 10¾-oz. can Campbell's Condensed Cream of Mushroom Soup
½ cup whole berry cranberry sauce
¼ cup orange juice

In skillet, cook bacon until crisp; remove and crumble. Pour off all but 2 Tbs. drippings. Cook celery and onion in drippings until tender. Toss lightly with stuffing mix, cornbread, broth, and egg. Fill cavity of turkey loosely with stuffing. Truss; place in roasting pan. Cover with foil. Roast at 325°F. for about 4 hours (25 minutes per pound or until tender). Uncover last hour to brown. Remove turkey to serving platter. Skim fat from drippings; add remaining ingredients. Heat; stir to loosen browned bits. Makes 12 servings.

Beer Batter Fish or Shrimp

A fast and fabulous batter from Bisquick® Baking Mix kitchens for fresh-caught or fresh-bought fish or shrimp.

Vegetable oil
1 lb. fish fillets or cooked large shrimp (or ½ lb. of each)
3 to 4 Tbs. Bisquick® Baking Mix
1 cup Bisquick® Baking Mix
½ tsp. salt
1 egg
½ cup beer

Heat vegetable oil (1½ inches) in heavy saucepan or deep fat fryer to 350°F. Cut fish in serving-size pieces. Lightly coat fish or shrimp with 3 to 4 Tbs. baking mix. Mix 1 cup baking mix, the salt, egg and beer until smooth. Dip fish or shrimp into batter, letting excess drip into bowl. Fry until golden brown, about 2 minutes on each side; drain. Makes 4 servings.

Boatman's Stew

Quick, easy and very "down east," this hearty fish soup was featured on the Hunt's Tomato Paste can back in the 1960's and is still a top favorite today.

2 lbs. firm-fleshed white fish (cod, haddock or
   halibut), cut in large chunks
   Salt
2 onions, sliced
2 Tbs. pure vegetable oil
1 6-oz. can Hunt's Tomato Paste
3 cups water
½ tsp. *each:* red pepper and black pepper
1 cup finely chopped parsley
⅓ cup dry white wine
6 slices of Italian bread (toasted, if desired)

Sprinkle fish with ½ tsp. salt; let stand 1 hour. Meanwhile, lightly brown onion in oil; pour off fat. Stir in Hunt's Tomato Paste, water, red pepper, 1½ tsps. salt, black pepper, parsley and wine. Simmer 20 minutes. Add fish; simmer about 10 minutes longer or just until fish flakes easily with a fork. To serve, place a slice of bread in each soup bowl; ladle soup over. Makes 6 servings.

Shrimp de Jonghe

Shrimp de Jonghe was created many years ago by Papa de Jonghe for the patrons of his popular Chicago restaurant. Although the restaurant is no longer in existence a never-fail version of this classic recipe has been developed by the Planters Peanut Oil expert cooks.

⅓ cup Planters Peanut Oil
½ cup flaked coconut
¼ cup fine dry bread crumbs
3 Tbs. chopped parsley
1 Tbs. minced garlic
¾ tsp. salt
¼ tsp. paprika
  Dash cayenne
2 pounds uncooked shrimp, shelled and
  deveined
½ cup sherry

Combine Planters Peanut Oil, coconut, bread crumbs, chopped parsley, minced garlic, salt, paprika and cayenne. Reserve about ¼ cup of mixture for topping. Toss shrimp lightly in remaining mixture until shrimp are well coated. Turn into lightly oiled 1½-quart casserole. Pour sherry over shrimp and sprinkle with reserved mixture. Bake, uncovered, in moderate oven (375°F.) until shrimp are tender. Makes 4–6 servings.

Avocados with Curried Chicken

This unusual dish was first featured in the Avocado Grower's advertising a decade ago. Everyone seemed to love it and it may have started the trend of serving avocado as a hot dish.

¼ cup butter (½ stick)
½ cup chopped, pared apple
¼ cup chopped onion
1 clove garlic, crushed
1 Tbs. curry powder
¼ cup flour
1 cup light cream
1 cup chicken bouillon

1 tsp. salt
⅛ tsp. pepper
2 cups cooked chicken, cut up or 1½ lbs. shrimp, cooked, shelled and cleaned.
3 or 4 avocados, halved and peeled
3–4 cups cooked rice
Condiments, given below

In saucepan: sauté apple, onion, garlic and curry powder in the butter until onion is crisp-tender. Stir in flour. Gradually add cream and bouillon; cook and stir until sauce boils 1 minute. Add salt, pepper and chicken or shrimp. Cook over low heat 10 minutes. Arrange avocado halves on rice in heatproof serving dish. Heat in 350°F. (moderate) oven for about 5 minutes. Spoon curried chicken or shrimp over avocado halves. Serve with Indian or Euphrates bread and a choice of these condiments: chopped egg, crumbled bacon, sweet mixed pickles, coconut, raisins, chutney, Bombay duck, preserved ginger, chopped peanuts. Makes 6–8 servings.

Stuffed Flounder Supreme

**Fish is America's latest "favorite food" but Wish-Bone®
printed this recipe on the label of their Deluxe French dressing more than ten years ago. Maybe it started the trend to
the ever-increasing popularity of fish.**

½ cup Wish-Bone® Deluxe French Dressing
1 lb. flounder fillets
¾ cup seasoned croutons, crushed
¼ cup finely chopped celery

Preheat oven to 350°F. Brush 2 Tbs. Wish-Bone® Deluxe French Dressing on top side of fillets. In small bowl, combine ¼ cup dressing, croutons, and celery; equally divide mixture on fillets and roll up. Brush fillets with remaining dressing and bake 35 minutes or until fish flakes. Makes about 4 servings.

Flounder Au Gratin

Back in my mother's family there was my cousin, John Jay, who served this elegant baked flounder, but wouldn't, for the longest time, tell me how he did it. John was a fine cook who enjoyed his reputation as a gourmet and he didn't want me to know it was so easy to prepare. It's a Hellmann's® Best Foods original.

¼ cup fine dry bread crumbs
¼ cup grated Parmesan cheese
 1 pound flounder or sole fillets
¼ cup Hellmann's® Best Foods Real Mayonnaise

In shallow dish or on sheet of waxed paper combine crumbs and cheese. Brush all sides of fillets with Real Mayonnaise; coat with crumb mixture. Arrange in single layer in shallow baking pan. Bake in 375°F. oven 20–25 minutes or until golden and fish flakes easily. Makes 4 servings.

Barbecued Red Snapper

A "cook out" or "cook in" favorite and definitely a Hunt-Wesson classic. This recipe first appeared on the Hunt Tomato Paste label in the 1950's.

2 lbs. red snapper steaks or fillets
1 6-oz. can Hunt's Tomato Paste
⅓ cup water
2 Tbs. lime juice
2 Tbs. Worcestershire sauce
1 Tbs. sugar
1 Tbs. Wesson oil
1 tsp. salt
⅛ tsp. garlic salt

Thaw fish if frozen; cut into serving-size portions. Combine remaining ingredients in a small bowl. Arrange fish on grill or broiler pan about 4 inches from heat source. Brush generously with sauce. Cook 6–10 minutes. Turn, brush with more sauce and cook 7–10 minutes longer or just until fish flakes when tested with a fork (length of cooking time depends on thickness of fish). Do not overcook. Makes 6 servings.

Imperial Fish Baltimore

A lovely, easy, inexpensive casserole from Lea & Perrins. Good enough for company, easy enough for every day.

3 Tbs. butter or margarine, divided
½ cup diced green pepper
¼ cup mayonnaise
2 tsps. Lea & Perrins Worcestershire Sauce
¼ tsp. salt
¼ tsp. powdered mustard
2 cups flaked cooked white fish

¾ cup soft bread crumbs
¼ cup chopped pimiento
½ tsp. paprika

In a medium saucepan melt 1 Tbs. of the butter. Add green pepper; sauté for 2 minutes. Remove from heat; stir in mayonnaise, Lea & Perrins, salt and mustard. Gently blend in fish. Turn into a buttered 1-quart casserole. In a small saucepan melt remaining 2 Tbs. butter. Stir in bread crumbs, pimiento, and paprika. Sprinkle over fish mixture. Bake in a preheated moderate oven (350°F.) until crumbs are golden, about 30 minutes. Makes 4 servings.

Stuffin'-Topped Halibut

Parkay published this easy way to transform frozen halibut steaks into a festive dish in their cookbook several years ago. It's a special favorite for Friday night supper.

2 cups soft bread crumbs
½ cup Squeeze Parkay Margarine
½ cup chopped celery
¼ cup chopped onion
¼ tsp. sage
¼ tsp. salt
4 frozen halibut steaks, ¾-inch thick (thawed)

Combine crumbs, margarine, celery, onion and seasonings; mix well. Place fish in 11¾ × 7½-inch baking dish; top with crumbs mixture. Bake at 350°F., 30–35 minutes or until crumbs mixture is golden brown and fish flakes easily with fork. Makes 4 servings.

Variations: Substitute salmon steaks for halibut. Substitute dill weed for sage.

Fish & Chips

I tell you those Crisco people know their deep-fried foods. This long-time "best ever" recipe pleases just about everybody. Some summer day serve it with a platter of tomatoes and cucumber slices, lemon-spiked iced tea and who knows, there may be fresh blueberry tart for dessert.

1 lb. fresh or frozen firm, white-fleshed fish fillets
1 lb. potatoes, peeled, (about 3 potatoes)
Crisco for deep frying
¼ cup flour
½ tsp. salt

1 egg yolk
2 Tbs. water
1 Tbs. Crisco, melted
1 egg white, stiffly beaten
¼ cup flour

Thaw fish, if frozen. Cut into serving-size pieces. Cut potatoes in uniform strips, slightly larger than for French fries. To make chips: Deep fry potato strips until golden brown in Crisco heated to 375°F. (about 7–8 minutes). Remove, drain on paper towels, and keep warm. In medium bowl, combine first ¼ cup flour and salt. Make well in center; add egg yolk, water, and melted Crisco. Stir until batter is smooth. Fold in egg white. Dip fish in the remaining ¼ cup flour, then into batter. Deep fry fish until golden brown in Crisco heated to 375° (about 1½ minutes on each side.) Sprinkle fish with vinegar, if desired. Sprinkle fish and chips with salt. Makes 3–4 servings.

Fillet of Sole en Croute

Here's the sort of recipe you'd expect to find in an expensive restaurant. Very special and very elegant indeed; but surprisingly easy. An immediate hit when it appeared on the Pepperidge Farm Frozen Puff Pastry package.

4 small fillets of sole
  Salt, pepper, thyme, tarragon
2 Tbs. butter or margarine
½ cup julienne onions
½ cup julienne mushrooms
½ cup julienne carrots
1 17¼-oz. package Pepperidge Farm Frozen
  "Bake It Fresh" Puff Pastry Sheets
1 egg, beaten

Sprinkle sole fillets lightly with salt, pepper, thyme and tarragon, and refrigerate. Melt butter in skillet; cut vegetables into narrow matchstick-like strips (julienne) and add to skillet. Season with salt and pepper and cook briefly, 3–5 minutes. Vegetables should remain crisp. Allow puff pastry sheets to thaw for 20 minutes, then unfold and cut each sheet into 4 squares. On a lightly floured surface, roll first square until it's slightly larger than the fillet. Place fillet in center of pastry, spoon ¼ cup of the julienne mixture on top. Roll second square of pastry only enough to cover sole fillet and border of the first sheet. Firmly press down edges to seal, trim excess with pastry wheel. If desired, use scraps to decorate pastry and attach with beaten egg. Repeat with remaining sole fillets and pastry. Place on baking sheet, brush top with beaten egg and bake in preheated 375°F. oven for 25–30 minutes or until golden brown. Makes 4 generous servings.

Teriyaki Fish Fillets

A California favorite from Kikkoman; light, lemony, refreshing. If you haven't already clipped and tried this one you must try it now.

⅓ cup Kikkoman Teriyaki Sauce
2 Tbs. lemon juice
1 Tbs. water
1 lb. fish fillets
⅓ cup thinly sliced green onions and tops

Combine teriyaki sauce with lemon juice and water. Place fish in single layer in shallow baking pan; pour teriyaki mixture over fish and marinate 5 minutes on each side. Bake fish in sauce in preheated 350°F. oven 10–15 minutes, or until fish flakes easily with fork. Remove fish onto serving platter, sprinkle with green onions and spoon sauce over all. Serve immediately. Makes 4 servings.

Batter-Fried Shrimp

Another Planters Peanut Oil winner, this is just the best recipe I've found for fried shrimp. The coating is crispy light, the shrimp cooked to pink perfection. The only thing wrong is that I have never been able to make enough.

2 lbs. uncooked shrimp, large
¾ cup unsifted flour
¾ cup water
1 egg, slightly beaten
1 Tbs. sugar
½ tsp. salt
  Planters Peanut Oil

Peel shrimp leaving tails on; devein. Split shrimp part way through, butterfly fashion. Combine flour, water, egg, sugar and salt to make a batter. Dip shrimp into batter and fry in deep, hot (375°F.) Planters Peanut Oil until golden brown. Drain on paper towels. Makes about 6 servings.

Tuna Croquettes

Now let me tell you there is nothing, no nothing, that can match the incredible goodness of a perfectly fried croquette, crisp and crunchy on the outside, meltingly delicious on the inside, and who knows better how to make croquettes than the cooks at Crisco!

3 Tbs. Crisco
¼ cup flour
⅔ cup milk
2 Tbs. finely chopped onion
1 Tbs. snipped parsley
2 tsps. lemon juice
¼ tsp. salt
   Dash pepper
   Dash paprika

2 6½ or 7-oz. cans tuna, drained and flaked
⅔ cup fine dry bread crumbs
1 egg, beaten
1 8-oz. package frozen peas with cream sauce
   Crisco for deep frying

In saucepan, melt the 3 Tbs. Crisco. Blend in the flour. Add the milk. Cook and stir till thickened and bubbly. Add the onion, parsley, lemon juice, salt, pepper and paprika; stir in the tuna. Cover and chill thoroughly, about 3 hours. With wet hands, shape tuna mixture into 8 cones, using about ¼ cup for each. Roll in crumbs. Dip into a mixture of beaten egg and 2 Tbs. water; roll in crumbs again. Prepare peas with cream sauce according to package directions; keep hot. Meanwhile, fry a few croquettes at a time till brown and hot in deep Crisco heated to 350°F., about 3 minutes. Drain on paper toweling. Spoon pea sauce over croquettes. Makes 4 servings.

Tuna Creole in Rice Ring

Tuna again? It can be a company treat when you turn it into something special with a flavorful creole sauce and serve it in a buttery rice ring. A top request recipe ever since it appeared on the Hunt's Tomato Paste can about ten years ago.

1 green pepper, chopped
½ cup chopped onion
½ cup sliced celery
1 clove garlic, crushed
2 Tbs. pure vegetable oil
1 6-oz. can Hunt's Tomato Paste
1¼ cups water

1 tsp. salt
1 tsp. dill weed
1 bay leaf
Dash Tabasco
2 6½ to 7-oz. cans chunk style tuna, drained and flaked
4 cups hot cooked rice

Sauté vegetables and garlic until tender in oil. Add Hunt's Tomato Paste, water and seasonings. Simmer 30 minutes, stirring occasionally. Stir in tuna; heat through. Pack hot cooked rice in buttered ring mold, turn out onto serving platter. Spoon tuna creole into center. Makes 4 servings.

Pasta, Pasta Americana!

Mueller's was the official supplier of pasta for the 1980 Olympic Winter games in Lake Placid. To celebrate they developed 80 new American-style recipes to be used on their packages. Here are four top winners.

Lake Placid Steak 'n' Peppers

1 lb. tender steak, very thinly sliced
¼ cup butter or margarine
1 large clove garlic, mashed
3 large onions, chopped
2 small green peppers, chopped
¼ cup dry sherry

¼ cup sliced pimiento
1 to 2 tsps. salt
½ tsp. pepper
8 oz. Mueller's Thin Spaghetti
2 Tbs. vegetable oil
Grated Parmesan cheese

In large skillet brown meat in butter with garlic; remove meat to warm platter. Add onion and green pepper to skillet and cook until crisp-tender; add sherry, pimiento and seasonings; return meat to skillet. Meanwhile, cook spaghetti as directed on package; drain. Toss spaghetti with oil, then combine with meat-vegetable mixture. Top with Parmesan cheese. Makes 4–6 servings.

Chalet Casserole

8 oz. Mueller's Thin
 Spaghetti
2 cups meatless spaghetti
 sauce
4 oz. thinly sliced pepperoni
1 4-oz. can mushroom stems
 and pieces, undrained

1 Tbs. grated onion
2 slices (4 oz.) Mozzarella
 cheese, cut in half
 diagonally

Cook spaghetti as directed on package; drain. In 11 × 8 × 2-inch baking dish combine spaghetti with sauce, pepperoni, mushrooms with liquid, and onion; top with cheese. Bake at 350°F. about 20 minutes or until bubbling. Makes 4 servings.

Frank-ly Fabulous Spaghetti

1 lb. frankfurters, cut in
 1-inch slices
½ cup chopped onion
¾ cup diced green pepper
2 Tbs. butter or margarine
2 8-oz. cans tomato sauce

½ tsp. chili powder
¼ tsp. ground cumin, if
 desired
⅓ cup sliced stuffed olives
8 oz. Mueller's Thin
 Spaghetti
 Grated Parmesan cheese

Cook frankfurters, onion and green pepper in butter until vegetables are tender. Stir in tomato sauce, chili powder and cumin. Simmer, covered, 20 minutes; stir occasionally. Add olives; heat. Meanwhile, cook spaghetti as directed on package; drain. Serve frankfurter sauce over spaghetti; sprinkle with Parmesan cheese. Makes 4–6 servings.

Unbelievable Lasagne

Lasagne originated in Italy, but you don't have to be Italian to make it. This short-cut method from Mueller's kitchens received its name (unbelievable) from the good American cooks who first tested the recipe. You don't have to pre-cook the lasagne and believe it or not it works!

4 to 5 cups spaghetti sauce
8 oz. lasagne
1 lb. Ricotta cheese

8 oz. Mozzarella cheese, shredded or thinly sliced
1 cup grated Parmesan cheese

In 13 × 9 × 2-inch baking pan, spread about 1 cup sauce; arrange a layer of uncooked lasagne; top with some sauce, Ricotta, Mozzarella, Parmesan and sauce. Repeat, gently pressing lasagne pieces into cheese mixture below. End with a final layer of lasagne; pour remaining sauce over, making sure all lasagne pieces are covered with sauce; top with remaining Mozzarella and Parmesan. (Do not be concerned with the empty space at the ends of the pan—during cooking the lasagne will expand and take up most of the area.) Bake at 350°F. for 45–55 minutes until lightly browned and bubbling. Allow to stand 15 minutes; cut in squares to serve. Serves 6–8.

Moon over Mostaccioli

We are told a romantically inclined member of the San Giorgio family came up with this intriguing name for what is surely one of the best pasta meals ever created.

2 Tbs. olive oil
2 Tbs. butter
½ cup finely chopped onion
½ cup finely chopped celery
1 medium green pepper, finely chopped
½ clove garlic, minced
¼ cup chopped stuffed olives
¼ cup chopped parsley
1 1-lb. jar San Giorgio Spaghetti Sauce with
   Meat
8 oz. (½ package) San Giorgio Mostaccioli Rigati
   (Pasta)
½ cup grated Cheddar cheese

Heat olive oil and butter in heavy saucepan. Sauté onion, celery, green pepper and garlic for 10 minutes. Add olives, parsley and sauce; simmer 10 minutes more. Meanwhile prepare mostaccioli according to package directions. Drain well. Toss with sauce in heated bowl. Sprinkle with Cheddar cheese. Serves 4.

Red Clam Sauce and Linguine

Traditional—and wonderful—a classic Italian dish that is on permanant file at the Hunt's Tomato Paste test kitchens.

1 onion, chopped
1 clove garlic, minced
2 Tbs. olive oil
2 6½-oz. cans minced clams, drained
1 6-oz. can Hunt's Tomato Paste

1 cup water
2 Tbs. lemon juice
1 Tbs. chopped fresh parsley
1 tsp. sugar
¼ tsp. rosemary
¼ tsp. ground thyme
8 oz. linguine or spaghetti, cooked and drained
Grated Parmesan cheese (optional)

Sauté onion and garlic in oil in skillet. Add clams and their juice, Hunt's Tomato Paste, water, lemon juice, parsley, sugar, rosemary and thyme. Simmer, uncovered, 15 minutes. Serve over cooked linguine; sprinkle with Parmesan, if desired. Makes 4 servings.

Fettuccini Carbonara

San Giorgio printed this classic but easy recipe for Fettuccini on their box label a dozen years ago and it's a truly marvelous tasting, low-cost dinner any night of the week.

¼ lb. bacon
1 12-oz. box San Giorgio Fettuccini
¼ cup butter or margarine, softened
½ cup heavy cream, at room temperature
½ cup grated Parmesan cheese
2 eggs, slightly beaten
2 Tbs. snipped parsley

Sauté bacon until crisp; drain well and crumble. Cook Fettuccini according to package directions. Drain well and place in warm serving dish large enough for tossing. Add crumbled bacon, butter, heavy cream, grated cheese, eggs and snipped parsley; toss until Fettuccini is well coated. Makes 6 servings.

Salmon Quiche

Recommended for this book by a number of excellent cooks as the best salmon quiche ever. It's from Castle and Cook Inc. who produce Bumble Bee® Pink Salmon.

- 1 10-inch unbaked pie shell
- 1 15½-oz. can Bumble Bee® Pink Salmon
- 1 9-oz. package frozen chopped spinach
- 1½ cups shredded Monterey Jack cheese
- 1 3-oz. package cream cheese, softened
- ½ tsp. salt
- ½ tsp. thyme
- 4 eggs, lightly beaten
- 1 cup milk

Preheat oven to 375°F. Bake pie shell 10 minutes until partially set. Drain salmon. Mash bones. Cook spinach according to package directions. Drain well. Combine spinach, Monterey Jack cheese, cream cheese, salt and thyme. Arrange salmon and mashed bones into pie shell. Spoon spinach mixture on top. Combine eggs and milk. Pour over salmon and spinach. Bake in preheated oven 40–45 minutes. Let stand 10 minutes before serving. Makes 6–8 servings.

Mexican Quiche

A French quiche with a Mexican Flavor? Of course that's what American cuisine is all about. We pick the best then combine them. The result? As delicious a dish as this "South of the Border" quiche from Pet-Ritz.®

- 1 Pet-Ritz® Regular Pie Crust Shell
- 1 4-oz. can Old El Paso Whole Chilies
- 6 slices bacon, cooked and drained
- 1 4-oz. cup Swiss cheese, shredded

3 eggs
1 cup light cream
¼ tsp. salt
Dash ground nutmeg

Preheat oven and cookie sheet to 425°F. Drain chilies and dry with toweling. Remove rib and seeds. Chop in large pieces. Crumble bacon and mix with chopped chilies. Sprinkle Swiss cheese on bottom of unbaked pie shell, then chilies and bacon. Mix together eggs, cream, salt and nutmeg. Slowly pour over cheese mixture. (The pie will be very full, but should not spill over.) Place on cookie sheet in preheated oven and bake for 15 minutes. Reduce temperature to 350°F. and bake an additional 20–25 minutes or until knife inserted in the center comes out clean. Cool 10–15 minutes before serving. Serves 6–8.

Savory Fish Pie

A classic down-east recipe from Blue Bonnet Margarine—perfect for a one-dish supper.

½ tsp. peppercorns
¼ tsp. tarragon leaves
1 bay leaf
1½ lbs. flounder fillets
½ lb. yellow onions, sliced
  Water
1 Tbs. finely diced pimiento
3 Tbs. Blue Bonnet Margarine
3 Tbs. flour
2 tsps. dry mustard
1¼ tsp. salt
⅛ tsp. pepper
¾ cup milk
1 tsp. Worcestershire sauce
¼ cup chopped parsley
3 cups prepared mashed potatoes
  Paprika

Tie peppercorns, tarragon and bay leaf in cheesecloth. Place in a large saucepan with fillets and onions. Cover with water. Bring to a boil. Reduce heat; simmer until onions are tender. Drain; reserve ¾ cup stock. Arrange fish and onions in 2-quart oblong dish. Scatter diced pimiento over fish. Melt Blue Bonnet Margarine in a small heavy saucepan. Blend in flour, dry mustard, salt and pepper. Cook over low heat, stirring, until smooth and bubbly. Remove from heat and stir in milk and Worcestershire sauce. Return to heat and bring to a boil, stirring constantly. Cook 1 minute longer. Stir in parsley, spoon sauce over fish. Top with mashed potatoes. Sprinkle with paprika. Bake in a hot oven (400°F.) for 30–35 minutes, or until potatoes are lightly browned and edges are bubbly. Makes 6 servings.

Breakfast Sausage Apple Pie

Meat for dessert? Pie for breakfast? Why not? New Englanders often served mince-meat tarts for a main course at suppertime, apple pie with pork for breakfast. Back in Depression days this pie made a great inexpensive breakfast, lunch or supper dish. It still does. From Oscar Mayer's test kitchen.

1 lb. Oscar Mayer Pork Sausage Links
1 11-oz. package pie crust mix
1 1 lb. 4-oz. can apple pie filling
1 cup (4 oz.) shredded processed American
   cheese
½ cup brown sugar, firmly packed

Cook pork sausage links; drain on paper towel. Meanwhile, use ½ package pie crust mix to prepare single pastry for 9-inch pie pan. Line pan with pastry; flute edge and prick bottom and sides with fork. Bake 10 minutes in 375°F. oven. Pour pie filling into partially baked shell; arrange cooked sausage, spoke fashion, on pie filling; sprinkle with shredded cheese. For topping, combine brown sugar with remaining pie crust mix; sprinkle over pie. Return to oven and bake 25–35 minutes or until crust is golden brown. Serve warm. Makes 6 servings.

Italian Zucchini Crescent Pie

A new $40,000 Grand Prize Pillsbury Bake-Off® winner; a beautifully seasoned vegetable-and-cheese main course dish that received its just due. You'll love it.

4 cups thinly sliced, unpeeled zucchini
1 cup coarsely chopped onion
¼ cup margarine or butter
½ cup chopped parsley or 2 Tbs. parsley flakes
½ tsp. salt
½ tsp. pepper
¼ tsp. garlic powder
¼ tsp. basil leaves
¼ tsp. oregano leaves
2 eggs, well beaten
8 oz. (2 cups) shredded natural Muenster or Mozzarella cheese
8 oz. can Pillsbury Refrigerated Quick Crescent Dinner Rolls
2 tsp. Dijon or prepared mustard

Heat oven to 375°F. In 10-inch skillet, cook zucchini and onion in margarine until tender, about 10 minutes. Stir in parsley and seasonings. In large bowl, blend eggs and cheese. Stir in vegetable mixture. Separate dough into 8 triangles. Place in ungreased 11-inch quiche, or 10-inch pie pan or 12 × 8-inch baking dish; press over bottom and up sides to form crust. Spread crust with mustard. Pour vegetable mixture evenly into crust. Bake at 375°F. for 18–20 minutes or until knife inserted near center comes out clean. (If crust becomes too brown, cover with foil during last 10 minutes of baking.) Let stand 10 minutes before serving. Cut into wedges. To reheat: cover loosely with foil, heat at 375°F. for 12–15 minutes.

Ham Corn Bread Pie

If you grew up in Texas as I did, you'll remember corn bread pies. Served like today's pizza, they were a favorite teenage party fare. This updated version was dreamed up by the good cooks at Planters Peanut Oil Test Kitchens.

2 Tbs. Fleischmann's Margarine
1 cup onion slices
1 large clove garlic, minced
¼ tsp. chili powder
½ cup Planters Cocktail Peanuts, chopped
   Generous dash pepper
1 10-oz. package corn bread mix
1 egg
½ cup milk
½ lb. sliced boiled ham
3 slices pasteurized processed American
   cheese, cut in half
2 pimiento-stuffed olives, sliced

Melt Fleischmann's Margarine in a large skillet. Add onions, garlic and chili powder. Cook over medium heat, stirring occasionally, until onions are tender. Remove from heat, stir in Planters Cocktail Peanuts and pepper.

Prepare corn bread mix according to package directions, using egg and milk. Spread on bottom of 12-inch pizza pan. Arrange ham on corn bread; top with onion mixture. Bake in hot oven (425°F.) 10 minutes. Top with cheese. Bake 5 minutes longer, or until cheese is melted. Garnish with olive slices. Makes 6–8 servings.

2.
Side Dishes: Potatoes, Rice, and Vegetables

Lately I've been having a grand time reading some very charming old books on food, filled with nostalgia and loaded with marvelous "receipts" that are endearing, but vague. Always enthusiastic about food, I was tempted to translate romance into reason and try out some of these seemingly enticing dishes. But what *sounds* good doesn't always come out the way the cook fondly imagines it would. Now after several sobering disasters of fallen cakes, soggy fried foods and gummy rice dishes, I bow to expertise and accuracy. And I treasure more than ever the recipes collected for this book—specific, accurate, easy-to-follow measurements and directions that guarantee success time after time after time. The recipes are inventive and imaginative too, but the ultimate test is THEY TASTE GOOD.

What has all this to do with side dishes? Simply this: side dishes are sometimes brushed off as unimportant, but if the juicy steak is accompanied with greasy, underdone French fries, the bloom is certainly off the rose. The perfect fish entree will be irretrievably marred by the gummy rice. Therefore, concise, accurate easy-to-follow recipes are at least as important to side dishes as they are to the main event. I believe you will find the side dishes included here to be added attractions to any meal, even "stars" in their own right—dishes to make with ease and enjoy with pleasure.

Thin and Crispy French Fries

French did I say? Perhaps by origin yes, but in this country no one vegetable is more universally loved than all-American crispy fries. Here's how to make the real thing. It's the famous Crisco recipe—on Crisco's label since 1938.

Use one or two medium-size potatoes per serving. Using knife or French-fry cutter, cut peeled potatoes into ¼-inch strips. Rinse or soak in cold water. Start heating enough Crisco Shortening to fill a 3-quart saucepan half full, or a deep fryer within ½ inch of the fill mark. Dry potato strips thoroughly on paper towel.

For extra quick French fries: Heat deep Crisco Shortening to 365°F. For electric deep fryer, follow manufacturer's directions for amount of potato strips to fry at one time. For saucepan, cook 2–3 cups of potato strips at one time, adding slowly. Cook until potatoes are tender and lightly browned, about 10–15 minutes. Drain potatoes on paper towel. While frying remaining potatoes, keep fried ones warm in oven set at low temperature. Salt or season as desired. If desired, frozen French fried potatoes can be used in place of fresh potatoes. For best results, fry about 10–15 minutes in Crisco Shortening using the above directions.

For extra crispy French fries (for fresh potatoes only): Fry potatoes *first* time at 325°F. for about 3 minutes. Remove and drain on paper towel. Cool at least 15 minutes at room temperature. If desired, cool for up to 3 hours. To serve, re-heat Crisco to 365°F. and fry potato strips a *second* time for 6–8 minutes or until golden brown. Drain on paper towel.

Cheese 'n' Cream Potatoes

Appi Watkins gives the best parties in town; her buffets are famous and they always include her special potato casserole. It took me years to discover the recipe came from Betty Crocker.

1 package Betty Crocker® Sour Cream 'n' Chive
 Potatoes
2 cups milk
3 eggs
½ tsp. salt
¼ tsp. pepper
1 cup shredded Mozzarella cheese (about 4 oz.)

Heat oven to 350°F. Grease 1½-quart round casserole. Cover potatoes with boiling water in small bowl. Let stand uncovered 10 minutes; drain thoroughly. Beat milk and eggs with hand beater. Mix all ingredients in casserole. Bake uncovered until potatoes are tender and top is golden brown, 45–50 minutes. Makes 6 servings.

Pennsylvania Dutch Potato Bake

At the Campbell test kitchens they tell me this is a very popular dish for buffet parties. Looks pretty and tastes grand, hot or at room temperature.

6 slices bacon
1 10¾-oz. can Campbell's Condensed
 Chicken Broth
2 Tbs. flour
¼ cup vinegar
2 Tbs. brown sugar
2 Tbs. diced pimiento
¼ cup diagonally sliced green onions
½ tsp. celery salt
¼ tsp. hot pepper sauce
6 cups cooked sliced potatoes

In skillet, cook bacon until crisp; remove. Pour off all but ¼ cup drippings. Gradually blend broth into flour until smooth; slowly stir into drippings. Add remaining ingredients except potatoes. Cook, stirring until thickened. In 1½-quart shallow baking dish (10 × 6 × 2 inches) arrange potatoes; pour broth mixture over potatoes. Cover; bake at 400°F. for 30 minutes. Garnish with bacon. Makes about 6 cups.

Pan-Fried Potatoes

Some of the best things you can eat are childishly simple to prepare—if you know how. You'll find the "know-how" for perfect pan-fried potatoes on the Crisco shortening label; but it's such a worthwhile thing to know I've included it here.

3 medium potatoes
  Salt and pepper
⅓ cup Crisco

Wash and peel the potatoes. Cut potatoes in ⅛-inch slices. Season with salt and pepper. In a covered skillet, fry potatoes in hot Crisco over medium heat for 10 minutes. Turn potatoes carefully. Cook, uncovered, about 10 minutes longer, loosening slices of potatoes occasionally and browning all sides. Makes 4 servings.

Herbed Potatoes: Prepare pan-fried potatoes as above. The last 5 minutes of cooking, sprinkle the fried potatoes with 2 Tbs. finely chopped celery, 2 Tbs. snipped fresh parsley, 2 Tbs. finely chopped onion, and ½ tsp. dried oregano, crushed. Sprinkle potatoes with salt and pepper to taste. Makes 4 servings.

Twice-Baked Potatoes

I love them—so do just about another million Americans who found the recipe, as I did, on the Campbell Cheddar Cheese Soup label.

8 medium baking potatoes
2 Tbs. butter or margarine
¼ tsp. salt
1 can Campbell's Cheddar Cheese Soup
1 Tbs. chopped dried chives

Bake potatoes until done. Cut potatoes in half lengthwise; scoop out insides leaving a thin shell. With electric mixer, mash potatoes with butter and salt. Gradually add soup and chives; beat until light and fluffy. Spoon into shells. Sprinkle with paprika. Bake in 2½-quart shallow baking dish (13 × 9 × 2 inches) at 450°F. for 15 minutes or until hot. Makes 8 servings.

Freckle-Faced 'Taters

I've been told that salt and butter are the perfect topping for potatoes, but melted butter plus grated cheese and bread crumbs seasoned not only with salt but also with Tabasco and Worcestershire is something to keep in mind.

2 large potatoes, baked
½ cup grated Cheddar cheese
4 Tbs. butter or margarine
2 Tbs. milk
¼ tsp. Tabasco Pepper Sauce
⅛ tsp. salt
1 tsp. Worcestershire sauce
½ cup crushed croutons or bread crumbs

Quarter hot potatoes lengthwise and place in a bake-and-serve dish. Sprinkle grated cheese over potatoes.

Melt butter in a skillet; add remaining ingredients, stirring until crushed croutons are moist. Crumble mixture over potatoes and place under broiler until cheese has browned. Makes 4 servings.

Spanish Rice

At Riviana Rice Company they tell me they put this recipe on the back of their box almost thirty years ago "just to show potatoes they weren't so indispensable after all." I guess they did all right. It's now a Southern classic.

  3 Tbs. bacon drippings
  1 cup uncooked Riviana Rice
  ¾ cup chopped onion
  ½ cup chopped green pepper
  ½ cup chopped celery
  1 14-oz. can stewed tomatoes
  1 cup water
1½ tsps. salt
  1 tsp. chili powder

Heat 2 Tbs. fat in large skillet; add rice. Brown lightly, stirring frequently. Add remaining 1 Tbs. fat, onion, green pepper and celery; cook until soft. Add remaining ingredients, cover pan tightly, and simmer for 20–30 minutes. If rice is then not sufficiently tender, add a little more water, cover, continue to cook until soft. Makes 6 servings (about ½ cup each).

Pilaf

Campbell put this Pilaf recipe on their beef broth can some fifteen years ago, and it's made millions of American meals "special" ever since.

½ cup fine noodles, broken in pieces
2 Tbs. butter or margarine
1 can Campbell's Beef Broth
⅓ cup water
½ cup raw long grain rice

In saucepan, brown noodles in butter; stir often. Add remaining ingredients. Bring to a boil; reduce heat. Cover; simmer 20–25 minutes, or until liquid is absorbed. Makes about 2½ cups.

Vegetables Sicily

A Parkay Margarine vegetable recipe which has been used many times in my kitchen and never fails to please, no matter who's been invited to supper.

3 cups zucchini slices
1 medium onion, sliced
1 tsp. oregano leaves, crushed
½ tsp. salt
¼ tsp. pepper
⅓ cup Parkay Margarine
1 medium tomato, cut into wedges

Sauté zucchini, onion, and seasoning in margarine. Add tomato; cook 5 minutes or until vegetables are tender. Makes 4–6 servings.

French-Style Vegetable Stew

From Heinz the most marvelous vegetable dish. It originated in France, but it's right at home on American tables.

1 cup chopped onions
2 cloves garlic, minced
2 small zucchini, thinly sliced
1 medium green pepper, cut into thin strips
½ cup olive or salad oil
1 medium eggplant, pared, cut into strips (2 × ½-inch)
3 Tbs. flour

4 medium tomatoes, peeled, cut into eighths
¼ cup Heinz Tomato Ketchup
1 Tbs. salt
1 tsp. Heinz Apple Cider Vinegar
½ tsp. crushed oregano leaves
¼ tsp. pepper

In Dutch oven, sauté first four ingredients in oil until onion is transparent. Coat eggplant with flour; add with tomatoes to sautéed vegetables. Combine ketchup and remaining ingredients; pour over vegetables. Cover; simmer 30–35 minutes; stir occasionally, or until vegetables are tender. Makes 8–10 servings (about 7 cups). NOTE: Zucchini may be peeled if skin is tough.

Sour Creamed Green Beans

You asked for that "other" green bean recipe, the one with sour cream. Well, there are dozens of variations on this theme, but here's one of the best from the Parkay Margarine test kitchens.

1 onion, thinly sliced
  Parkay margarine
2 10-oz. packages frozen green beans, thawed, drained

1 cup dairy sour cream
¼ cup flour
1½ tsps. salt
¼ tsp. pepper
1 cup (4 oz.) shredded Kraft sharp natural
   Cheddar cheese
1 cup soft bread crumbs

Sauté onion in ¼ cup margarine. Add to combined beans, sour cream, flour and seasonings; mix lightly. Pour into greased 1½-quart casserole. Sprinkle with cheese; top with crumbs tossed with ¼ cup melted margarine. Bake at 350°F. 25 minutes. Makes 4–6 servings.

Green Beans Polonaise

Is there anything elegant that can be done with a can of green beans? The cooks at Del Monte tell me there most certainly is and this is it.

1 16-oz. can Del Monte Whole or Cut Green
   Beans
3 Tbs. butter
1 clove garlic
2 Tbs. instant minced onion
3 Tbs. fine dry bread crumbs
   Few drops lemon juice

In oven-proof dish, heat green beans in 300°F. oven. Melt butter over low heat. Set aside until milk solids have settled to bottom. Skim off clarified butter discarding solids. Rub skillet with garlic. Heat clarified butter until browned. Sauté onion and add bread crumbs and lemon juice. Cook until browned, being careful not to burn crumbs. Drain beans, keep warm. Top with buttered bread crumbs. Makes four servings.

Golden Capped Baked Tomatoes

Sun-ripened, home-grown tomatoes and this recipe from the R. T. French Company can make your reputation next summer as the best cook in town.

6 medium-size tomatoes
  Salt and pepper to taste
¼ cup mayonnaise
1 Tbs. French's Prepared Mustard
1 tsp. French's Minced Onion
½ tsp. sugar
2 Tbs. fine dry bread crumbs

Cut each tomato in half. Place cut side up in a shallow baking dish; sprinkle cut surface with salt and pepper. Combine the remaining ingredients. Spoon a portion on top of each tomato; spread to cover cut surface.* Bake in 400°F. oven 15 minutes or until topping is lightly puffed and tomatoes are hot. Makes 6 servings.

* Can be prepared in advance to this point. Refrigerate until ready to begin baking. Baking time may need to be increased slightly.

Tomato Sour Cream Casserole

Daisy Doolin, mother of Elmer Doolin (the man who invented Fritos® Corn Chips), came up with this super recipe years ago. She made it with Fritos® Corn Chips. Now it's even zippier with Doritos® Tortilla Chips. Easy and filling, it's a great inexpensive dish.

1 medium onion, chopped
2 Tbs. salad oil
1 1-lb. 12-oz. can tomatoes
1 package Mexican style "sloppy joe"
   seasoning mix
1 4-oz. can green chilies, chopped
1 5½-oz. package Doritos® Nacho Cheese
   Tortilla Chips, slightly crushed
¾ pound Monterey Jack cheese, grated
1 cup sour cream
½ cup grated Cheddar cheese

Sauté onion in oil; add tomatoes, seasoning mix and green chilies. Simmer, uncovered, 10–15 minutes. In greased, deep 2-quart casserole, layer ingredients in the following order: sauce, crushed Doritos® Tortilla Chips, Monterey Jack cheese, sauce, Monterey Jack cheese. Top with sour cream. Bake at 325°F. for 30 minutes. Sprinkle with Cheddar cheese; bake 10 minutes longer. Makes 6–8 servings.

Elegant Puffed Broccoli

An original from Hellmann's® Best Foods who tell me it was one of the first recipes devised in their test kitchens to use this puffy broiled topping.

2 bunches broccoli, cut into spears or 2 10-oz.
   packages frozen broccoli spears, cooked,
   drained
2 egg whites, at room temperature
¼ tsp. salt
½ cup shredded Swiss cheese (2 oz.)
½ cup Hellmann's® Best Foods Real Mayonnaise

Arrange hot cooked broccoli in shallow 1½-quart pan or broiler proof serving dish. In small bowl with mixer at high speed beat egg whites and salt until stiff peaks form. Fold in cheese and mayonnaise; spoon evenly over broccoli. Broil 6 inches from source of heat 4 minutes or until golden brown. Serve immediately. Makes 6–8 servings.

Candy-Coated Carrots

Remember this sweet way to persuade you to eat your vegetables? The Tabasco people tell me good cooks have been using their recipe for what will soon be four generations.

4 Tbs. butter or margarine
4 Tbs. brown sugar
¼ tsp. Tabasco Pepper Sauce
⅛ tsp. salt
1 tsp. lemon juice
6–8 carrots, sliced and cooked

Place butter and brown sugar in a saucepan over medium heat, stir until combined. Add Tabasco and salt; mix well; add lemon juice. Remove from heat. Add hot, drained carrots and toss gently until coated evenly. Makes 4 servings.

Triple Corn Fritters

Back in 1960 the Green Giant test kitchens developed this super good version of an American classic. It's the best of the best; just perfect for a 1981 Sunday special breakfast or supper.

1⅓ cups Pillsbury's Best® All-Purpose or
    Unbleached Flour*
½ cup yellow cornmeal
1 Tbs. baking powder
2 tsps. sugar
1 tsp. salt
2 eggs, beaten
⅓ cup milk
2 Tbs. oil
1 8½-oz. can Green Giant Brand Golden
    Cream Style Corn
1 12-oz. can Green Giant Niblets Brand Golden
    Whole Kernel Corn, drained
    Oil for deep frying

Lightly spoon flour into measuring cup; level off. In medium bowl, combine flour, cornmeal, baking powder, sugar and salt. In large bowl, combine eggs, milk, oil and cream style corn. Blend in dry ingredients, stirring just until moistened. Stir in whole kernel corn. In deep fat fryer or heavy saucepan drop batter by tablespoonfuls and fry in 2–3 inches hot fat (365°F.) for 2–3 minutes on each side or until golden brown. Drain on paper towel. Serve warm. Makes 28 fritters.

TIP: *Self-rising flour is not recommended.

Now-You-Like-'em Greens

And you will even if you never liked spinach before. It's this cream cheese sauce from Tabasco that does it.

3 lbs. (or 3 bunches) fresh spinach, cooked
¼ tsp. Tabasco Pepper Sauce
½ tsp. salt
4 Tbs. butter or margarine
1 3-oz. package cream cheese
2 Tbs. milk
2 hard-cooked eggs, sliced or ⅔ cup bread
   crumbs.

To hot, drained spinach, add Tabasco, salt, butter, and cream cheese that has been softened with milk. Stir until butter has melted and ingredients are blended. Place in a casserole and bake for 10 minutes at 375°F. Garnish with egg slices or bread crumbs. Makes 6 servings.

New England Harvest Baked Beans

Several years ago this recipe won a contest sponsored by B & M Brick Oven Baked Beans. Chopped apples are the surprise ingredient and it tastes divine.

2 28-oz. cans B & M Brick Oven Baked Beans
½ cup catsup or barbecue sauce
½ cup cider vinegar
½ cup maple syrup
¼ cup brown sugar
1 Tbs. dry mustard
2 cups baking apples (peeled, cored and cubed)
¼ to ½ lb. bacon

Preheat oven to 350°F. In a 3-quart baking dish, mix together B & M Brick Oven Baked Beans, catsup, vinegar, maple syrup, brown sugar, dry mustard and baking apples. Arrange bacon slices over top of casserole. Bake uncovered, for 45 minutes. Makes 8 servings.

Beans Hawaiian

You don't have to be a vegetarian to enjoy this flavorful meatless bean recipe from Heinz. For my taste, it's just perfect with cold sliced leftover baked ham.

    2 1-lb. cans Heinz Vegetarian Beans in Tomato
       Sauce
   *1 8-oz. can pineapple chunks, drained
  1–2 Tbs. light brown sugar
  1½ tsps. Heinz Mild Mustard
   ¼ tsp. salt
       Dash ground cloves

Combine ingredients; pour into a 1-quart casserole. Bake, uncovered in 375°F. oven, 50–55 minutes or until beans are hot, stirring occasionally. Makes 4–6 servings (about 4 cups).

* 1 8½-oz. can pineapple slices, drained and cut into chunks may be substituted.

3.
All-American
Sauces

Sparkle—that's what a good sauce lends to the dish at hand. Now the French have long been regarded as the masters of sauce-making but they had best look to their laurels, for here are real American-made, American-born, sauces to transfer so-so dishes into super ones. For example, if you would make the most of leftover meat, try one of the trio of sauces from Pepperidge Farm; turn those fresh-cooked, but dull, green beans or broccoli into a treat with Tabasco's special cream and mayonnaise sauce, or surprise yourself with a barbecue sauce made with strained baby food—that's right, baby food!

All our sauces are "asked for" specials featured by food companies on their labels and in their advertising. They are indeed "tried and true," easy, expert and extra special. And why not? All the skill and resources of trained and talented cooks went into their creation, and each is just that, a creation in its own right.

Continental Lemon Sauce

This has been dressing up vegetables, broiled fish, even poached eggs since 1965; as spectacularly good as hollandaise but a lot easier. It's from Hellmann's® Best Foods.

1 cup Hellmann's® Best Foods Real Mayonnaise
2 eggs
3 Tbs. lemon juice
½ tsp. salt
½ tsp. dry mustard

In small saucepan with wire whisk beat all ingredients until smooth. Stirring constantly, cook over medium-low heat until thick (do not boil). Serve over vegetables, seafood or poached eggs. Sprinkle with paprika. Makes 1⅔ cups.

Burgundy Steak Sauce à la Worcester

You don't have to serve a sirloin steak to enjoy this sauce, though it's nice. Try it over plain grilled hamburger. Fabulous!

2 Tbs. butter or margarine
¼ cup chopped onion
2 10½-oz. cans beef gravy
3 Tbs. Burgundy or other dry red wine
4 tsp. Lea & Perrins Worcestershire Sauce
2 Tbs. chopped parsley

In a small saucepan melt butter. Add onion; sauté for 3 minutes. Stir in gravy, wine and Lea & Perrins. Cook and stir until hot, about 2 minutes. Stir in parsley. Serve hot over steak or hamburgers. Makes approximately 3 cups.

Hunt's Hawaiian Sauce

A very popular sauce with a very special flavor. Another American sauce original from Hunt's.

¼ cup brown sugar, packed
2 tsps. cornstarch
1 8-oz. can Hunt's Tomato Sauce
1 8½-oz. can crushed pineapple, undrained
1 Tbs. lemon juice
1 Tbs. minced crystallized ginger
¼ tsp. onion salt
¼ tsp. garlic salt
⅛ tsp. pepper

Blend brown sugar and cornstarch in 1-quart saucepan. Add remaining ingredients; blend thoroughly. Bring to a boil, stirring. Lower heat; cover, simmer gently 15–20 minutes. Stir occasionally. Use as a basting or serving sauce for chicken, ribs, meatballs. Makes 2 cups.

Hunt's Quick Spaghetti Sauce

A very special sauce from Hunt's Tomato Sauce Cookbook which is a collection of all-time favorites from Hunt's Products labels. The book was compiled in response to consumers who complained "they were running out of space to store the cans" or "never got to copy the recipe before the can was thrown away."

½ lb. ground beef
3 8-oz. cans Hunt's Tomato Sauce
½ cup water
1 2-oz. can sliced mushrooms, drained
2 Tbs. minced onion flakes
1½ tsp. brown sugar, packed
¾ tsp. oregano
½ tsp. basil
½ tsp. garlic salt
⅛ tsp. marjoram

Sauté ground beef in skillet; drain fat. Add remaining ingredients. Heat to boiling. Simmer 10 minutes. Stir occasionally. Serve over hot cooked spaghetti or other pasta. Makes 4 servings.

Come-and-Get-It Sauce for Vegetables

This is such an elegant but easy way to sauce a vegetable you'll wonder why you didn't think of it yourself. The Tabasco Pepper Sauce people did way back in 1950.

1 cup sour cream
¼ cup mayonnaise
2 Tbs. lemon juice
½ tsp. salt
¼ tsp. Tabasco Pepper Sauce

Combine all ingredients in a saucepan and heat gently; do not allow to boil. Spoon over vegetable when serving, or place vegetable in a casserole, top with sauce, sprinkle with bread crumbs, and place under broiler until crumbs are brown, 1–2 minutes. Ideal with cooked fresh asparagus, or broccoli, cabbage, cauliflower, green beans, etc. Sauce for 4–6 servings.

THREE SUPER SAUCES FROM PEPPERIDGE FARM

Pepperidge Farm developed these special sauces for hot sandwiches to make the most of their soft Family Rolls and leftover meats. Just split and heat rolls, cover with room-temperature sliced meat, top with bubbly hot sauce and serve at once.

Beef Barbecue Sauce

2 Tbs. butter or margarine
1 large onion, chopped
1 cup chili sauce
½ cup beer
½ cup sliced stuffed olives

Combine all ingredients in a saucepan and simmer for 5 minutes or until flavors are blended. Makes 1½ cups sauce.

Apple and Raisin Sauce for Ham

1 cup apple sauce
½ cup apple butter
½ cup raisins
½ cup maple syrup

Combine all ingredients in a saucepan and simmer until bubbly. Makes 2¼ cups.

Curried Sauce for Turkey or Chicken

¼ cup butter or margarine
1 clove garlic, chopped
1 onion, chopped
1 apple, peeled, cored and chopped
1 tsp. curry powder
¼ cup flour
1 cup chicken broth
1 cup (½ pint) light cream
   Salt and pepper

In a saucepan, melt butter and sauté garlic, onion and apple for 5 minutes. Stir in curry powder and sauté for 1 minute more. Stir in flour and gradually add chicken broth and cream. Stir over low heat until sauce bubbles and thickens. Season to taste and add salt and pepper. Serve with cooked sliced turkey or chicken. Makes 2 cups.

Barbecue Sauce for Hot Dogs

Best recipes sometimes come from the most surprising places. This one from the Gerber people who, as I'm sure you know, make excellent baby food.

1 7¾-oz. jar Gerber Junior Peach Cobbler
⅓ cup catsup
⅓ cup vinegar
⅓ cup brown sugar
1 clove garlic, minced
1 Tbs. Worcestershire sauce
½ tsp. ginger
¼ tsp. mace
1 tsp. onion salt

Combine all ingredients thoroughly. Score hot dogs

diagonally on three sides. Barbecue, basting with sauce about three times while cooking. Makes 1½ cups sauce (enough for 2 lbs. of hot dogs).

Variations: Use on pork or chicken. Use heated sauce in chafing dish with sliced hot dogs.

Worcestershire Butter Sauce

Simple, but simply elegant. It's sauces like this that separate the chefs from the cooks.

½ cup butter or margarine
1 Tbs. chopped parsley
2 Tbs. lemon juice

1½ tsp. Lea & Perrins Worcestershire Sauce
⅛ tsp. salt

In a small saucepan melt butter. Stir in remaining ingredients. Heat thoroughly. Serve over fish or vegetables.

Texas Barbecue Sauce

English Lea & Perrins Worcestershire Sauce goes western for the best barbecue you'll ever eat.

1 5-oz. bottle Lea & Perrins Worcestershire Sauce
2 cups water
1 cup cider vinegar
¾ cup lemon juice
¼ cup oil

¼ cup firmly packed brown sugar
2 tsps. salt
1 tsp. garlic salt
½ tsp. ground black pepper

In a medium saucepan combine all ingredients. Bring to boiling point. Reduce heat and simmer, uncovered for 10 minutes. Cool. Pour into tightly covered container. This sauce will keep refrigerated for several weeks. Use for chicken, hamburgers or steak. Makes 4 cups.

Horseradish Sauce

Now I will tell you how to make a beef eater happy and still keep your budget in line. Cook up some inexpensive beef short ribs, then serve them with this horseradish sauce from Hellmann's® Best Foods. Or serve with sliced meats, such as tongue, ham or cold cuts.

1½ cups Hellmann's® Best Foods Real
    Mayonnaise
¼ cup prepared horseradish, drained
2 Tbs. light corn syrup
2 Tbs. dry sherry or tarragon vinegar
2 tsps. prepared mustard
¼ tsp. hot pepper sauce
⅛ tsp. salt

In small bowl stir together all ingredients. Cover; chill. Makes 2 cups.

In 1921 the Mazola Company produced a cookbook featuring Mazola Oil. It was endorsed by Oscar of the Waldorf—a famous chef of that time. In it were two of his own original sauces. Today these sauces are classics; used by good cooks all over the world.

Delmonico Sauce

½ cup plain French
  dressing
1 tsp. tomato catsup
1 tsp. Worcestershire sauce

¼ tsp. finely chopped green
  peppers
1 hard-boiled egg finely
  chopped or rubbed
  through a sieve.

Mix all ingredients and serve on freshly cooked broccoli or green beans, or use as a superb salad dressing on crisp greens.

Tartar Sauce

1 cup of mayonnaise
2 Tbs. of capers
2 Tbs. of olives
2 Tbs. of gherkins
1 Tbs. of parsley
¼ tsp. of onion juice or finely chopped shallots or
  white onions

Chop capers, olives, gherkins, and parsley very fine. Fold into the mayonnaise and serve cold. Serve with fried fish or cold seafood.

Seafood Cocktail Sauce

Another American original. This recipe was perfected by Creole cooks on Avery Island in Louisiana where they make Tabasco Pepper Sauce.

1 Tbs. prepared horseradish
1 Tbs. Worcestershire sauce
3 Tbs. catsup
¼ tsp. Tabasco Pepper Sauce
1 Tbs. lemon juice
¼ tsp. salt

Mix ingredients thoroughly. Makes 4 very small servings.

4.
Salads
and
Their Dressings

You know, I would particularly enjoy stamping out all those so-called "salad bars," the ones featuring 33 kinds of pickles, some tired iceberg lettuce and a few wilted tomatoes.

On the other hand the *right* salad rounds out the meal, enhances and highlights the main course, adds lightness and contrast and—no small consideration—contributes greatly to the nutritional quality of your meal with all the vitamins and minerals fresh fruits and vegetables contain.

Sometimes the salad *is* the meal, needing only good bread and iced tea or coffee for a light but satisfying luncheon or supper.

The trick of course, is to put as much imagination and just plain "good cookery" into your salads as any other dish you prepare and that's just what our test-kitchen experts have done for you in the pages to follow. Interesting and delicious, easy and quick, each one is a worthwhile addition to your recipe file.

You may, in fact, already have some of these recipes—most are old favorites from labels or advertising—but if you've lost or mislaid your copies, here they are, good, good tasting, and good for you as any salad should be.

P.S. We didn't forget the dressing either; included are a bevy of really good ones to transform even old standby lettuce and tomato into something special, and to turn great salad into sublime eating.

Macaroni Supper Salad

I bet you never thought of putting Hunt's Tomato Sauce in a salad, but what goes better than tomato sauce with macaroni?

1 8-oz. pkg. small shell macaroni
2 cups diced cooked ham or luncheon meat
½ cup coarsely grated raw carrot
¼ cup chopped onion
¼ cup chopped green pepper
1 tsp. salt
1 cup mayonnaise or salad dressing
1 8-oz. can Hunt's Tomato Sauce

Cook, drain and rinse macaroni according to package directions. Mix with ham, carrots, onion, green pepper and salt in large bowl. Blend mayonnaise and Hunt's Sauce in small bowl. Pour over salad ingredients; toss lightly to mix. Chill thoroughly. Serve on crisp salad greens. Makes 6 servings.

Chutney Ham Salad

Highly recommended by trustworthy friends who are also trustworthy cooks who obtained the recipe from the trusty people at Dole's test kitchens.

1 1-lb. 4-oz. can Dole Chunk Pineapple in Juice
2 cups diced ham
1 cup shredded Cheddar cheese
  Crisp salad greens
1 cup dairy sour cream
3 Tbs. chutney

Drain pineapple, reserving 2 Tbs. juice. Arrange pineapple, ham and cheese onto each of four salad plates lined with crisp salad greens. For dressing, combine sour cream, reserved juice and chutney. Spoon over each salad to serve. Makes 4 servings.

Sesame Salmon Boats

Add another great and different main course salad to your collection. It makes very good use of Bumble Bee® Red Salmon. If you like salmon, you'll be pleased.

1 7¾-oz. can Bumble Bee® Red Salmon
1 avocado
   Crisp salad greens
   Lemon juice
¼ cup mayonnaise
¼ tsp. dill weed
¼ tsp. garlic salt
2 tsps. toasted sesame seeds

Drain salmon. Remove skin, if desired. Mash bones. Halve avocado; remove seed. Place each half on a salad plate lined with crisp salad greens. Sprinkle with lemon juice. Combine mayonnaise, dill weed, garlic salt and 1 tsp. sesame seeds. Fold in salmon and mashed bones. Spoon into avocado halves. Sprinkle with remaining sesame seeds to serve. Makes 2 servings.

Crisp and Crunchy Tuna

Dole Pineapple and Bumble Bee® Tuna make all-American tuna salad a star-spangled special.

1 1-lb. 4-oz. can Dole Sliced Pineapple in Juice
1 7-oz. can Bumble Bee® Solid White Albacore
   Tuna, drained
1 11-oz. can mandarin orange segments,
   drained

1 medium cucumber, peeled, scored and sliced
¼ cup chopped green onion
   Crisp salad greens
1 cup mayonnaise
1 Tbs. lemon juice
¼ tsp. curry powder

Drain pineapple, reserving 2 Tbs. juice. Break large chunks of tuna with a spoon. Toss tuna, oranges, cucumber and green onion. Spoon onto each of 5 salad plates lined with crisp salad greens. Arrange 2 slices pineapple over each. Combine reserved juice, mayonnaise, lemon juice and curry. Spoon over each salad to serve. Makes 5 servings.

Italian Bean Salad

The seasoning is Italian, but it's one of America's favorite salads—from Hellmann's® Best Foods.

1 6-oz. envelope Italian dressing mix
¼ cup cider vinegar
1 9-oz. package frozen Italian green beans,
   cooked, drained
1 16-oz. can chick peas, drained
1 7-oz. can pitted ripe olives, drained
1 cup sliced celery
1 small red onion, thinly sliced
½ cup Hellmann's® Best Foods Real Mayonnaise

In medium bowl stir together dressing mix and vinegar. Add next 5 ingredients; toss to coat well. Cover; chill overnight. Just before serving, toss salad with Real Mayonnaise. Makes 6–8 servings.

All-American Macaroni Salad

What backporch supper was ever complete without it? Cold cuts, ice, and coconut cake for dessert. Memories are made of such menus.

½ cup Hellmann's® Best Foods Real Mayonnaise
1 tsp. prepared mustard
¼ tsp. salt
⅛ tsp. pepper
1 cup elbow macaroni (4 oz.), cooked, drained
½ lb. frankfurters, sliced
¼ cup cubed processed American cheese
¼ cup sliced green onions (optional)

In large bowl stir together first 4 ingredients. Add remaining ingredients; toss to coat well. Cover; chill at least 2 hours. Makes 4 cups.

California Sliced Vegetable Salad

This Hollywood-style salad was the star of a recent Lea & Perrins Worcestershire Sauce advertisement. It's a beautiful addition to any menu.

2 ripe avocados, peeled, pitted, and sliced
2 ripe tomatoes, sliced
1 red onion, thinly sliced
⅓ cup oil
1 Tbs. Lea & Perrins Worcestershire Sauce
1 Tbs. lemon juice
1 tsp. basil leaves, crumbled
1 tsp. salt
½ tsp. sugar
2 Tbs. chopped parsley

On a shallow platter alternately arrange avocado, tomato and onion slices, one slice overlapping the next. In a small container combine remaining ingredients except parsley. Mix well. Pour over vegetables. Cover and refrigerate for 1 hour. Sprinkle with parsley and serve. Makes 6 servings.

Corn 'n' Cucumbers

Even in the dead of winter you'll find the ingredients for this salad very easy to come by. It features Del Monte canned kernel corn, thinly sliced cucumbers and a tangy sauce.

 2 medium cucumbers
½ medium onion
 1 17-oz. can Del Monte Whole Kernel Family
   Style Corn
½ cup white distilled vinegar
 2 Tbs. sugar
 2 Tbs. water
 1 tsp. dill weed
¼ tsp. pepper
   Dash cayenne pepper
   Parsley sprigs

Peel and thinly slice cucumbers and onion. Drain corn, reserving liquid for other recipe uses. Combine all other ingredients except parsley. Pour over cucumbers, onion and corn in salad bowl. Chill. Toss and garnish with parsley sprigs.

Country-Style Cole Slaw

This cole slaw reminds me of Mary Eisenman. Mary lived next door to me in Shreveport, Louisiana, and was famous for her cold fried chicken and cole slaw Sunday night suppers. She probably got the cole slaw recipe from Hellmann's® Best Foods as I did.

½ cup Hellmann's® Best Foods Real
    Mayonnaise
2 Tbs. sugar
2 Tbs. cider vinegar
¾ tsp. salt
¼ tsp. dry mustard
⅛ tsp. celery seeds
4 cups coarsely shredded cabbage
¾ cup coarsely shredded carrots
½ cup diced green pepper
2 Tbs. sliced green onions

In medium bowl stir together first 6 ingredients. Add remaining ingredients; toss to coat well. Cover; chill at least 2 hours. Makes 4 cups.

Acapulco Salad

This is a special salad, very special indeed. Served with your own homemade enchiladas and ice cold beer, it's not just supper, it's a fiesta.

1 2¼-oz. can sliced ripe olives
1 8½-oz. can garbanzo beans
1 8¾-oz. can Del Monte Whole Kernel Family
    Style Corn
½ head iceberg lettuce
1 bunch radishes
    Bottled green goddess dressing
    Garlic salt and pepper to taste
    Shredded cheddar cheese

Drain olives, garbanzo beans and corn. Using sharp knife, shred lettuce, and thinly slice radishes. Toss ingredients with dressing. Garnish with garlic salt, pepper and cheddar cheese.

Ensalada Verde

This is an all-green salad—verdant and cool—in a Spanish marinade and with a garlic salsa.

2 avocados, peeled, pitted and sliced
½ cup olive or salad oil
2 Tbs. vinegar
1 clove garlic, halved
1 tsp. each: dry mustard, salt
¼ tsp. pepper
1 cup pimiento-stuffed olives
1 package each: frozen Italian green beans,
    French-style green beans, green peas,
    asparagus spears—all cooked and drained
1 large cucumber, peeled and thinly sliced
    Salsa Aioli (below)

Combine for marinade: oil, vinegar and seasonings. Beat or shake well. Arrange avocados, olives and vegetables in serving dish. Pour marinade over vegetables and chill several hours. Makes 6–8 servings.

Salsa Aioli: Crush 6 cloves garlic; beat in 2 egg yolks. With fork or wire whisk, slowly beat in 1 cup olive oil and juice of 1 lemon. Add salt and pepper to taste. Makes about 1 cup.

Avocado and Mushroom Salad

This elegancy of avocados and raw white mushrooms is marinated in wine, greened with parsley and spiced with fresh pepper. A lovely accompaniment to a rich main dish.

⅓ cup olive oil
1 Tbs. white wine vinegar or white wine
1 Tbs. chopped parsley
1 clove garlic, halved

1 tsp. salt
 Fresh ground black pepper
 Juice of 1 lemon
2 avocados, peeled, pitted and thinly sliced
½ lb. mushrooms, thinly sliced
 Parsley, for garnish

Combine and chill for marinade: oil, vinegar, seasonings and lemon juice. Layer sliced avocados and mushrooms on platter. Marinate in dressing 1 hour. Makes 6–8 servings.

Waldorf Salad à la Russe

Waldorf salad goes Russian with the addition of sour cream and Wish-Bone® Russian Dressing.

¼ cup Wish-Bone® Russian Dressing
¼ cup dairy sour cream
1 cup diced apple
1 cup diced celery
½ cup chopped walnuts

In medium bowl, blend Wish-Bone® Russian Dressing with sour cream. Add apple, celery and walnuts; toss together. If desired, serve in lettuce cups. Makes about 4 servings.

Garden Fresh Salad

The "can't-be-improved," original, creamy smooth gelatine salad with crunchy vegetables. It's from the Knox Unflavored Gelatine package and surely belongs in every good cook's recipe file.

2 envelopes Knox Unflavored Gelatine
2 Tbs. sugar
1½ cups boiling water
1 cup mayonnaise
¼ cup Wish-Bone® Italian Dressing
3 Tbs. lemon juice
Suggested Vegetables*

In large bowl, mix Unflavored Gelatine with sugar; add boiling water and stir until Gelatine is completely dissolved. With wire whisk or rotary beater, blend in mayonnaise, Italian dressing and lemon juice; chill, stirring occasionally, until mixture is the consistency of unbeaten egg whites. Fold in suggested Vegetables. Turn into 8-inch round or square baking pan; chill until firm. To serve, cut into wedges or squares. Makes about 8 servings.

* Suggested Vegetables: Use any combination of the following to equal 2 cups; Chopped tomato, celery, radishes, mushrooms, asparagus or cucumbers.

Summer Salad with Sour Cream Dressing

This is one of those especially Southern salad ideas that was handed down from one generation to the next and then passed on from friend to friend until no one quite remembers the original recipe. This version was perfected by the good cooks at the Tabasco Pepper Sauce kitchens.

2 tsps. unflavored gelatin
  Sour Cream Dressing (below)
¼ cup cold water
2 cups cottage cheese
1 cup (¼ pound) crumbled blue cheese
½ cup mayonnaise
2 Tbs. minced scallion
1 tsp. Tabasco Red Hot Pepper Sauce
½ cup heavy cream, whipped
3 cups cut-up fresh fruit in season
  (melon balls, strawberries, pear strips, citrus sections, etc.)
6 lettuce cups

Sprinkle gelatin over water; stir over hot water until gelatin is dissolved. Combine cheeses; blend in gelatin. Stir mayonnaise, scallion and Tabasco into cheese mixture until all ingredients are thoroughly blended. Fold whipped cream into cheese. Pour into lightly oiled quart mold. Chill until firm, about 4 hours. Carefully unmold cheese salad onto plate. Surround mold with individual fruit salads in lettuce cups. Serve with Sour Cream Dressing.

Sour Cream Dressing:

1 cup sour cream
1 Tbs. mayonnaise

¼ tsp. Tabasco Red
  Hot Pepper Sauce

Combine all ingredients. Refrigerate until ready to serve. Makes 6 servings.

Salmon Dill Mousse

A buffet party special salad. It's been a favorite recipe since Jell-O first introduced it back in the 1930's.

    2 3-oz. packages or 1 6-oz. package Jell-O
      Lemon Gelatin
    2 cups boiling water
    1 cup cold water
    3 Tbs. lemon juice
    1 1-lb. can pink salmon, drained and flaked
    ½ cup sour cream
    ¼ cup mayonnaise
    2 Tbs. minced onions
  1½ tsp. dill weed

Dissolve gelatin in boiling water. Add cold water and lemon juice. Chill until thickened. Mix salmon with remaining ingredients. Blend into thickened gelatin. Pour into an 8 × 4-inch loaf pan. Chill until firm—about 4 hours. Unmold. Garnish with dill and thinly sliced cucumber, if desired. Makes 5⅓ cups or 6—8 servings.

Beets in a Mustard Ring

This buffet supper salad mold recipe was created by special request from a Midwest consumer who asked Standard Brands Test Kitchens for "a mustard ring mold like the one that was always served at church suppers when I was a girl."

  4 eggs
  ¼ cup white vinegar
  ¼ cup sugar
  1 Tbs. dry mustard

½ tsp. salt
1 3-oz. package Royal Lemon Gelatin
¾ cup boiling water
1 cup heavy cream, whipped
   Small whole pickled beets

Break eggs in top of double boiler and beat until foamy. Add vinegar, sugar, dry mustard and salt; blend well. Dissolve Royal Lemon Gelatin in boiling water, add to egg mixture and cook over simmering water, stirring frequently, until mixture is of custard consistency. Cool. Fold whipped cream into cooled mixture. Pour into a 5-cup ring mold and chill until firm. To serve, unmold and fill center with pickled beets. Makes 8–10 servings.

California Fruit Salad Rosé

From Knox Unflavored Gelatine this is a delicate combination of wine and fruit that's extra easy to prepare. It's been featured on their package since 1965.

1 envelope Knox Unflavored Gelatine
2 Tbs. sugar
¾ cup boiling water
1¼ cups rosé wine
1 cup thinly sliced peaches
½ cup sliced bananas
½ cup sliced strawberries

In medium bowl, mix Unflavored Gelatine with sugar; add boiling water and stir until Gelatine is completely dissolved. Stir in wine. Chill, stirring occasionally, until mixture is consistency of unbeaten egg whites. Fold in peaches, bananas and strawberries. Turn into 4-cup mold or bowl and chill until firm. Makes about 6 servings.

Iberia French Dressing

It's the bit of sugar and the peppery hot Tabasco that give this time-honored French dressing its American accent.

⅔ cup salad oil
⅓ cup lemon juice or vinegar
½ tsp. Tabasco Pepper Sauce
1 tsp. each salt, paprika, dry mustard
½ tsp. sugar

Combine ingredients and shake well in covered jar. Shake well before using. Makes 1 cup dressing.

Variations: To ½ cup Iberia French Dressing add:

Roquefort Dressing: 1–2 Tbs. Roquefort cheese, crumbled.

Chive Dressing: 1–2 Tbs. chopped chives or green onion.

Herb Dressing: 2 tsps. chopped parsley, ⅛ tsp. thyme, ½ tsp. oregano.

Creole Dressing: ¼ cup catsup, ½ tsp. Worcestershire sauce.

Vinaigrette Dressing: 1 hard-cooked egg, chopped, 2 Tbs. chopped green pepper, 1 Tbs. grated onion.

Hot Dan's Dressing

The R. T. French Company printed this creamy hot sauce on the mustard jar several years ago; it's a sure-fire way to transform potato salad, cole slaw and deviled eggs into an epicurean feast.

¼ cup French's Prepared Mustard
2 Tbs. sugar
2 Tbs. vinegar
2 Tbs. half-and-half or undiluted evaporated milk
¼ tsp. salt

Combine all ingredients; beat with rotary beater until light and fluffy. Makes ½ cup.

YOGURT DRESSINGS

I can't track down just exactly who dreamed up yogurt dressing, but I'm told this winning combination originated in California. Dannon was the first to print the recipe. It's another American original that has become a national favorite.

Fruit Yogurt Dressing

Cool, creamy Yogurt Dressing is perfect for fruit salad.

½ cup Hellmann's® Best Foods Real Mayonnaise
1 8-oz. container flavored Dannon Yogurt

Fold mayonnaise into yogurt. Cover; chill. Makes 1½ cups.

Blue Cheese Dressing

Very special on sliced tomatoes or as a dip with raw vegetables.

⅓ cup mayonnaise
⅓ cup crumbled blue cheese
1 cup plain Dannon Yogurt

In small bowl, mix mayonnaise and blue cheese. Fold in yogurt. Cover and chill until serving time. Makes about 1½ cups.

Family French Dressing

This is that well beloved French dressing from Heinz that originated back in the 1920's. Your mother, no doubt, made it; mine did, and I still love it. So will you.

½ cup Heinz Tomato Ketchup
½ cup salad oil
¼ cup Heinz Apple Cider Vinegar
2 tsps. confectioners' sugar
1 clove garlic, split
¼ tsp. salt
  Dash pepper

Combine ingredients in jar. Cover; shake vigorously. Chill to blend flavors. Remove garlic; shake again before serving. Makes 1¼ cups.

Green Goddess Dressing

This creamy mixture dresses cold seafood as well as green salads.

1 cup Hellmann's® Best Foods Real Mayonnaise
½ cup parsley sprigs
2 green onions, cut up
2 Tbs. tarragon vinegar
2 tsps. sugar
¼ tsp. salt
¼ tsp. dry mustard
⅛ tsp. garlic powder
⅛ tsp. pepper
½ cup plain yogurt

Place first 9 ingredients in blender container; cover. Blend until smooth. Fold in yogurt. Cover; chill. Makes 1½ cups.

Louis Dressing

A California original. Great over cooked shrimp, tomato slices or hard cooked eggs.

1 cup Hellmann's® Best Foods
  Real Mayonnaise
½ cup spinach leaves
5 watercress sprigs
½ small onion
1 small clove garlic
1 Tbs. lemon juice
1½ tsps. sugar

Place all ingredients in blender container; cover. Blend until smooth. Cover; chill. Makes 1¼ cups.

Low Calorie Blue Cheese Dressing

The Tabasco people ran this recipe in an ad a few years ago and I tried it then. I had to include it here because (weight watchers take note) it's one of the best.

1 8-oz. can tomato sauce
2 Tbs. catsup
4 tsps. lemon juice
1 tsp. grated onion
¼ tsp. Tabasco Hot Pepper Sauce
½ tsp. salt
¼ cup crumbled blue cheese

Blend together all ingredients except blue cheese. Stir in blue cheese. Serve with salad greens. Makes 1⅓ cups (25 calories per Tbs.).

Peanut Butter Dressing

One of the most popular recipes from the Skippy Peanut Butter kitchens is this one for fruit salad dressing.

½ cup Skippy Super Chunk Peanut Butter
½ cup Karo Dark corn syrup
½ cup milk

In small bowl stir together peanut butter and corn syrup until blended. Stir in milk. Cover; refrigerate. Serve over fresh fruit. Makes about 1⅓ cups.

5.
Afterthoughts—
Snacks
and Such

Most cookbooks lead off with appetizers, but now really how many of us prepare appetizers as a preamble to everyday dinner? Not too many I would guess, so I started this cookbook with the real issue of the day—the main dishes to answer that endless question: What's for dinner? But for those special dinners, parties and occasions when you want to embellish a meal, here are some favorite recipes for snacks and dips, canapés, and hors d'oeuvres.

These are fun foods, fun to make and fun to eat; our test-kitchen friends have given us their best imaginative ideas for old favorites like popcorn turned into festive fare with little time, effort or money, dips of all kinds from mild to spicy-sharp cheese balls and spreads, canapés and pâtés. There's even a brand-new idea for vegetable appetizers to make with a mix.

Here is just what you need for your next cocktail party or for transforming that "stop by for a drink" invitation into something "special." Recipes to put a little extra enjoyment into life—each one easy, quick and light on the budget. Some are often requested old friends, some are new, but every one is a tested success, planned to make your entertaining life easier and more fun. Enjoy them!

Oriental Ham Tidbits

Armour cooks dreamed this one up a dozen years ago and they are still getting requests for the recipe. It's "nothing-to-it" easy and it is downright irresistible.

1 cup plum or red currant jelly
½ cup lemon juice
2 Tbs. cornstarch
1 lb. Golden Star Ham by Armour, cut into
    ¾-inch cubes
1 8-oz. can water chestnuts, drained, cut in half
1 green pepper, cut into 1-inch chunks

In large skillet, combine jelly, lemon juice and cornstarch. Heat, stirring constantly, until thickened. Add ham, water chestnuts and green pepper, stirring to coat pieces; heat through. Serve with wooden picks. Makes 5 cups.

Barbecued Cocktail Franks

This was said to have originated in Texas. It could have been, but Hunt's was first to print the recipe. Perhaps you should double the recipe.

1 6-oz. can Hunt's Tomato Paste
2 cups water
2 Tbs. *each*: minced onion, Worcestershire
    sauce and brown sugar
1 Tbs. *each*: white vinegar and molasses
1 tsp. *each*: lemon juice and dry mustard
½ tsp. salt
1 lb. cocktail frankfurters.

In a large saucepan, combine all ingredients except frankfurters. Bring to boil, stirring frequently; reduce heat. Add franks; simmer 10 minutes. Serve with toothpicks. Makes 32 appetizers.

Horseradish Dip

From a can of Bumble Bee® Pink Salmon an especially flavorful and different dip.

1 15½-oz. can Bumble Bee® Pink Salmon
1 8-oz. package cream cheese, softened
¼ cup dairy sour cream
¼ cup horseradish
½ tsp. salt
⅛ tsp. garlic powder
   Crisp romaine lettuce
   Paprika
   Crackers
   Celery sticks

Drain salmon. Remove skin, if desired. Mash bones. Beat cream cheese, sour cream, horseradish, salt and garlic powder until smooth. Beat in salmon and bones until blended. Arrange romaine lettuce in a bowl. Spoon in salmon mixture. Sprinkle with paprika. Serve with crackers and celery sticks. Makes 6–8 servings.

Hot Chili-Cheese Dip

A South-of-the-Border original from Armour, zesty with flavor, this dip is a firmly established favorite that pleases just about everybody.

1 15-oz. can Armour Star Chili (no beans)
1 4-oz. can chopped green chilies
1 lb. processed American cheese, shredded
1 Tbs. Worcestershire sauce
   Corn chips

Combine all ingredients, except chips; heat, stirring occasionally, over low heat until cheese melts. Serve heated as a dip with chips. Makes 4 cups.

Liptauer Spread

Kraft tells me this simple but simply fabulous spread has won rave notices ever since it appeared in their advertising fifteen years ago.

1 8-oz. package Philadelphia Brand Cream
  Cheese
½ cup soft Parkay Margarine
2 Tbs. finely chopped onion
1½ tsps. anchovy paste
1 tsp. Kraft Pure Prepared Mustard
1 tsp. capers, chopped
1 tsp. caraway seed
1 tsp. paprika

Combine softened cream cheese and margarine, mixing until well blended. Add remaining ingredients; mix well. Chill. Serve as a spread with French or pumpernickel bread. Makes 1½ cups.

These festive cheese balls are as tempting and delicious today as they were when Lea & Perrins created them years ago.

Coventry Cheese Ball

1 8-oz. package cream
  cheese, softened
1 cup (4 oz.) shredded
  sharp Cheddar cheese
¼ cup minced onion

2 Tbs. minced parsley
1 tsp. Lea & Perrins
  Worcestershire Sauce
¼ tsp. salt

In a bowl blend cream and Cheddar cheeses. Add onion, parsley, Lea & Perrins, and salt; blend well. Shape into a ball. Chill and serve with assorted crackers, if desired. Makes 1 cheese ball.

Harlequin Cheese Ball: Add 2 Tbs. finely diced pimiento, 1 tsp. prepared brown mustard, and 1 clove garlic, crushed, to basic cheese mixture. Shape into a ball. Chill. Garnish with pimiento stars, if desired.

Holiday Cheese Ball: Add 1 Tbs. caraway to basic cheese mixture. Shape into a ball. Chill. Sprinkle ribbons of paprika and chopped parsley around ball.

Fruit and Nut Cheese Ball: Add 1 8¼-oz. can crushed pineapple, well drained, and ⅓ cup finely chopped nuts to basic cheese mixture. Shape into a ball; roll in ⅓ cup finely chopped nuts. Chill.

Chicken Liver Paté

Planters Peanut Oil Company thought up this paté to make your entertaining life easy—and successful. I stir in about 2 Tbs. of good brandy, but I leave that up to you; it's great either way.

½ cup Planters Peanut Oil	1 hard-cooked egg
½ cup diced onion	1 tsp. salt
1 lb. cooked chicken livers	⅛ tsp. pepper

Heat Planters Peanut Oil in a heavy skillet; add diced onion and sauté until transparent, about 5 minutes. Allow to cool in skillet. Grind or chop together chicken livers, egg and entire contents of skillet. Stir in salt and pepper. Chill until ready to serve. Makes about 1½ cups spread.

Bacon-Onion Pinwheels

Remember these? The recipe appeared in a Kraft advertisement fifteen years ago. It's high on the list of Kraft's "most wanted" recipes.

½ cup finely chopped onion
⅓ cup soft Parkay Margarine
6 crisply cooked bacon slices, crumbled
2 Tbs. chopped parsley
2 8-oz. cans Pillsbury's® Refrigerated
  Quick-Crescent Dinner Rolls

Combine onion, margarine, bacon and parsley; mix well. Separate dough into eight rectangles; firmly press perforations to seal. Spread margarine mixture over dough. Roll up each rectangle, starting at short end; cut into four slices. Place on ungreased cookie sheet, cut-side down; flatten slightly. Bake at 375°F; 15–20 minutes or until golden brown. Makes approximately 2½ dozen.

From the Bisquick "No Time to Cook" summer recipe book here are two appetizers that get raves whenever they are served:

Zucchini Appetizers

3 cups thinly sliced
  unpared zucchini (about
  4 small)
1 cup Bisquick baking mix
½ cup finely chopped onion
½ cup grated Parmesan
  cheese
2 Tbs. snipped parsley
½ tsp. salt

½ tsp. seasoned salt
½ tsp. dried marjoram or
  oregano leaves
Dash of pepper
1 clove garlic, finely
  chopped
½ cup vegetable oil
4 eggs, slightly beaten

Heat oven to 350°F. Grease oblong pan, 13 × 9 × 2 inches. Mix all ingredients; spread in pan. Bake until golden brown, about 25 minutes. Cut into about 2- × 1-inch pieces. Makes 4 dozen appetizers.

Mushroom-Cheese Appetizers

2 cups Bisquick baking mix
½ cup cold water
¼ lb. bulk pork sausage
¼ cup finely chopped green onions (with tops)

¾ cup mayonnaise or salad dressing
35 medium mushrooms (about 1 lb.)
2 cups shredded Cheddar cheese (about 8 oz.)
Paprika

Heat oven to 350°F. Grease oblong pan, 13 × 9 × 2 inches. Mix baking mix and water until soft dough forms; beat vigorously 20 strokes. Press dough in bottom of pan with floured hands. Cook and stir sausage in skillet until brown; drain. Mix sausage, onions and mayonnaise. Remove stems from mushrooms. Finely chop stems; stir into sausage mixture. Fill mushroom caps with sausage mixture. Place mushrooms in rows on dough in pan; sprinkle with cheese and paprika. Cover pan loosely with aluminum foil. Bake 20 minutes; remove foil. Bake until cheese is bubbly, 5–10 minutes. Let stand 15 minutes; cut into pieces. Makes 35 appetizers.

Barbecued Korean-Style Short Ribs

Adapted by Kikkoman, this authentic Korean recipe is a West Coast favorite.

    4 lbs. pre-cut beef short ribs, 2½ inches long
    ½ cup Kikkoman Soy Sauce
    ¼ cup water
    1 Tbs. sugar
    1 Tbs. sesame seed, toasted
    1 tsp. Tabasco Pepper Sauce
    ½ tsp. garlic powder

Score meaty side of ribs, ½ inch apart, ½ inch deep, lengthwise and crosswise. Combine remaining ingredients. Marinate ribs in sauce in plastic bag 2 hours. Broil 2 inches from heat 15 minutes, or until ribs are brown and crisp on all sides.

Sweet-and-Sour Franks

You just wouldn't believe a humble frankfurter could taste so elegant. No wonder this quickie has been a Lea & Perrins "asked-for" recipe for years.

    ½ cup red currant jelly
    ½ cup prepared brown mustard
    2 Tbs. minced onion
    1 Tbs. Lea & Perrins Worcestershire Sauce
    1 lb. frankfurters, cut into 1-inch chunks

In a medium saucepan mix jelly, mustard, onion and Lea & Perrins; bring to boiling point. Add frankfurters; return to boiling point. Reduce heat and simmer, covered, for 15 minutes, stirring occasionally. If desired, serve hot from a chafing dish with cocktail picks. Makes about 32 hors d'oeuvres.

Seasoned Pop Corn

Trust American know-how, especially when it comes to casual entertaining. For casual entertaining at its best (and easiest) here are a few ideas from Jolly Time Pop Corn.

Blue Cheese Pop Corn: Melt 1 cup butter or margarine. Stir in 1 package blue cheese salad dressing mix. Toss with 6 quarts freshly popped Jolly Time Pop Corn.

Parmesan Pop Corn: Melt ¼ cup butter. Pour over 2 quarts popped Jolly Time Pop Corn. Add ½ cup grated Parmesan cheese and ½ tsp. salt. Mix well.

Herb Seasoned Pop Corn: Melt 3 Tbs. butter or margarine. Stir in ½ tsp. salt. Combine 1 tsp. thyme, ½ tsp. basil, ½ tsp. oregano and ½ tsp. rosemary. Add to butter. Pour over 2 quarts freshly popped Jolly Time Pop Corn. Toss well.

Curry Seasoned Pop Corn: Melt 3 Tbs. butter or margarine. Stir in ½ tsp. salt, 1 tsp. curry powder, ¼ tsp. ground cinnamon, and ¼ tsp. ground ginger. Toss with 2 quarts popped Jolly Time Pop Corn.

Flavored Pop Corn: Sprinkle one or more of the following over hot buttered Jolly Time Pop Corn:

Garlic salt	Chili powder	Butter flavored
Celery salt	Grated American	salt
Seasoned salt	cheese	Bacon-flavored
Hickory flavored	Dry soup mix	bits
salt	Dill weed	

Party Mix

2 quarts popped Jolly Time Pop Corn
2 cups slim pretzel sticks
2 cups cheese curls
½ tsp. seasoned salt
¼ cup butter or margarine
1 Tbs. Worcestershire sauce
½ tsp. garlic salt

In a shallow baking pan, mix popped corn, pretzel sticks and cheese curls. Melt butter or margarine in small saucepan and stir in seasonings. Pour over dry ingredients and mix well. Bake at 250°F. for about 45 minutes, stirring several times. Makes about 2½ quarts. NOTE: 1 cup dry roasted peanuts may be added.

Crispy Snack

3 quarts unsalted, popped Jolly Time Pop Corn
¼ cup butter or margarine, melted
½ 3¼-oz. can French fried onions
¼ cup bacon bits or bacon-flavored bits
   Salt to taste

Toss popped corn with melted butter. Stir in French fried onions and bacon bits. Sprinkle with salt. Place mixture on a jelly roll pan or baking sheet. Heat in 250°F. oven 5 minutes, serve hot.

Bacon-Cheese Pop Corn

4 quarts popped Jolly Time
 Pop Corn
⅓ cup butter or margarine,
 melted
½ tsp. seasoned salt

½ tsp. hickory-smoked salt
⅓ cup grated Parmesan or
 American cheese
⅓ cup bacon-flavored bits

Pour freshly popped pop corn in a large bowl. Combine butter with seasoned hickory-smoked salt. Pour over pop corn; toss well to coat. Sprinkle with cheese and bacon bits. Toss again and serve while warm.

Curry Party Mix

A new twist to that old favorite Chex® Party Mix. It's great for party snacking, but did you know it makes a perfect accompaniment to any curry dish? Inexpensive too!

½ cup butter or margarine
1¼ tsps. seasoned salt
1¼ − 2 tsps. curry powder
4½ tsps. Worcestershire sauce
2 cups Corn Chex® cereal
2 cups Rice Chex® cereal
2 cups Wheat Chex® cereal
2 cups Bran Chex® cereal
1 cup chow mein noodles
1 cup golden raisins

Preheat oven to 250°F. Heat butter in large shallow roasting pan (about 15 × 10 × 2 inches) in oven until melted. Remove. Stir in seasonings. Add Chex, noodles, and raisins. Mix until all pieces are coated. Heat in oven 1 hour. Stir every 15 minutes. Spread on absorbent paper to cool. Makes about 10 cups.

Chex® No-Cook Party Mix

Perfect for parties; this party mix is also great for children's after-school snacks. Tastes so good they won't know how good for them it really is.

1 cup Corn Chex® cereal
1 cup Rice Chex® cereal
1 cup Wheat Chex® cereal
1 cup Bran Chex® cereal
2 cups cheese-flavored corn puff balls
¾ cup broken pretzel sticks
1 cup peanut butter–flavored chips

Mix all ingredients together. Store tightly covered. Makes about 7 cups.

6.
Sandwiches

We eat sandwiches for lunch, pack them in school boxes, serve them at parties, make a meal of them; in short, we love sandwiches.

Fortunately, our food companies are just as fond of sandwiches as the customers, for their test kitchens continue to come up with fresh variations on old favorites as well as totally new combinations of sandwich "fixin's." Included here are the very special favorites, the asked-for recipes—sandwiches so popular the recipes are kept in permanent files to be sent out over and over to the customers who apparently never get enough good sandwich ideas.

I hope you will give the sandwich meal its just due; a good sandwich can, and should be, a meal in itself. Add a beverage, perhaps a good dessert and you have the makings of a perfect lunch or supper.

Now a few tips from the experts that I pass onto you with pleasure: A thin layer of softened butter, spread on cold, almost frozen bread, keeps a moist filling from making a soggy sandwich. Varied breads add to sandwich pleasure; homey-tasting whole wheat makes a great ham sandwich, English muffins are a pleasant change for hamburgers, and all sorts of buns can replace ordinary breads. Don't forget the relishes—pickles of course, for most sandwiches, but sometimes a sweet touch is great, too. Watermelons pickled with ham or tongue, cranberry sauce for turkey or chicken, and a couple of plump ripe olives added to a hamburger taste delicious. Sandwiches are also good garnished with cherry tomatoes or sticks of crisp cucumber and celery. The idea is to serve your sandwiches with imagination, with *verve!* That's what makes the difference.

Balboa Party Burgers

A Kraft "classic" and a very fancy burger. If there were a contest for the best possible burger, this would be my choice.

½ cup Kraft Real
  Mayonnaise
½ cup dairy sour cream
½ cup finely chopped onion
2 Tbs. chopped parsley
2 lbs. ground beef
  Salt and pepper

1 cup (4 ozs.) shredded Kraft
  Sharp Cheddar Cheese
6 rye bread slices, toasted
  Soft margarine
  Lettuce
2 large tomatoes, sliced

Combine mayonnaise, sour cream, onion and parsley; mix well. Shape meat into six oval patties. Broil on both sides to desired doneness. Season with salt and pepper. Top patties with sauce and cheese; broil until cheese is melted. Spread toast with margarine; top with lettuce, tomato and patties. Makes 6 servings.

Hamburgers Rancheros

Ever since the West was won, campfire cooks have known how good a spicy tomato sauce tasted over broiled meat. Here's an updated version with a special touch from Del Monte.

4 slices bacon, snipped
1 15-oz. can Del Monte Tomato Sauce
½ tsp. chili powder
½ tsp. garlic powder

2 Tbs. instant minced onion
¼ tsp. salt
¼ tsp. pepper
15 pitted green olives
1½ lbs. ground beef

Cook bacon and drain. Reserve 2 Tbs. drippings. Mix together in saucepan: tomato sauce, chili powder, garlic powder, onion, salt and pepper. Simmer 15 minutes. Halve the olives. Form beef into 4 patties and broil. Top with sauce, olives and bacon pieces.

Boston Burgers

Remember these? A 1930's favorite from Kraft and a real budget stretcher that tastes just as great now as way back then.

½ lb. ground beef
¼ cup chopped onion
1 22-oz. can baked beans
¼ cup chili sauce
½ tsp. salt
   Dash of pepper
8 hamburger buns, split, toasted
1 4-oz. pkg. Kraft Shredded Sharp Cheddar
   Cheese

Brown meat; drain. Add onion; cook until tender. Stir in beans, chili sauce and seasonings. Cover; simmer 20 minutes. Fill buns with meat mixture and cheese. Makes 8 sandwiches.

Piñata Burgers

Pita (pocket) bread sandwiches were big news in the 1970s. This one, from the R. T. French Company, is a smash hit every time it's served.

½ ripe avocado, diced or ½ cup chopped
   zucchini
1 medium-sized tomato, chopped
3– 4 Tbs. French's Worcestershire Sauce
1 Tbs. salad oil
1 tsp. lemon juice or vinegar
1 tsp. French's Parsley Flakes
1¼ tsps. French's Onion Salt
2 lbs. ground beef
6 small loaves pita (pocket) bread

Combine avocado, tomato, 1 Tbs. of the Worcestershire sauce, oil, lemon juice, parsley flakes, and ¼ tsp. of onion salt. Mix remaining 2 or 3 Tbs. Worcestershire and 1 tsp. of onion salt with the ground beef; form into 12 thin patties.* Place a spoonful of drained avocado mixture in center of 6 patties; top with remaining 6 patties and press edges together with a fork to seal. Grill over hot coals for about 10 minutes, turning once. Brush with liquid drained from avocado mixture while grilling. Slit outer edge of pita bread half way around and insert burger. Makes 6 servings.

* *Hint:* To easily form thin patties of uniform size, place a large square piece of plastic wrap over the inside of a plastic 1-lb. coffee can lid. Press enough ground beef into the lid to completely fill it, packing firmly. Carefully lift out the plastic wrap and place formed patty on a platter. Repeat process for each patty.

Tuna Bunwiches

Americans have been eating tuna sandwiches since way back when tuna was first put into cans. It's not what you call new—but a tuna bunwich with chopped peanuts and cream cheese and French's Prepared Mustard—now that's news!

1 3-oz. package cream cheese, softened
2 Tbs. French's Prepared Mustard
1 7-oz. can tuna, drained
½ cup finely chopped celery
¼ cup chopped peanuts
6 hamburger rolls
  Tomato slices
  Lettuce

Beat together cream cheese and mustard until smooth; stir in tuna, celery, and peanuts. Spread on rolls; top with tomato and lettuce. Makes 6 servings.

Scotchburgers

New Pepperidge Farm Puff Pastry Sheets, an old recipe for "penny pies" sold on the streets of Aberdeen, Scotland, as far back as the eighteenth century, add up to a great new hot or cold sandwich idea.

1 17¼-oz. package Pepperidge Farm Frozen
  "Bake It Fresh" Puff Pastry Sheets
2 lbs. lean ground beef
½ cup chopped celery
2 Tbs. instant minced onion
¼ cup chopped parsley
¼ tsp. sage
¼ tsp. salt
⅛ tsp. pepper
1 cup Pepperidge Farm Corn Bread Stuffing
¼ cup plain yogurt or sour cream
1 egg, beaten

Thaw pastry 20 minutes, then unfold sheets. Cut each sheet into 4 squares. In a large mixing bowl, thoroughly mix beef, celery, onion, parsley, sage, salt, pepper and stuffing. Stir in yogurt or sour cream until mixture is bound together. Shape mixture into 8 generous size meat patties. Broil patties on each side for 3– 4 minutes or until brown. Cool. Drain on paper towels. On a lightly floured board, roll out each square of pastry about 1½ inches larger than meat patties. Set the patties in center of square and fold pastry over meat, sealing edges in the center. Place seam side down on a baking sheet and brush with beaten egg. Bake in preheated oven (400°F.) for 20 minutes. Serve hot or cold. Makes 8 servings.

Sausage and Pepper Filled Deli Rolls

Pepperidge Farm kitchens adapted this Italian hero-style sandwich for their packaged Deli rolls. Serve them with a jug of red wine and you're in Italy.

1½ lbs. sweet Italian sausage
1 clove garlic, chopped
2 red onions, sliced thinly
2 red peppers, seeded and cut into thin strips
2 green peppers, seeded and cut into thin strips
3 tomatoes, chopped
1 tsp. oregano
Salt and pepper
1 11-oz. package Pepperidge Farm Deli Rolls

Slice sausages in ½-inch thick crosswise slices. Fry sausage in a skillet until brown and cooked; remove from skillet. Add garlic, onions and peppers to pan drippings. Sauté for 5– 6 minutes or until vegetables are tender but still crisp. Add tomatoes and oregano and simmer 5– 6 minutes or until tomatoes are cooked. Season to taste with salt and pepper. Split roll and fill with sausage filling. Serve at once with plenty of napkins. Makes 6 servings.

The Original Brunch-wich

This super flavorful hot sandwich was the star of a recent series of advertisements from Underwood. It's just perfect for a festive brunch or luncheon party.

1 4½-oz. can Underwood Deviled Ham
2 English muffins, split, toasted
4 eggs, poached
4 slices, your favorite cheese

Spread deviled ham on each muffin half; top with poached egg. Lay cheese slice over each muffin. Broil 3–4 minutes until cheese is melted. Makes 4 servings.

Pizza Brunch-wich

Another brunch-wich from Underwood? I just couldn't resist it—you won't either when you bite into this combination.

1 4½-oz. can Underwood Deviled Ham
2 English muffins, split, toasted
4 eggs
¼ cup water
2 Tbs. butter or margarine
½ cup spaghetti sauce
2 slices Mozzarella cheese, halved

Spread deviled ham on each toasted muffin half. In small bowl, beat eggs with water. In medium skillet, melt butter; add eggs and cook, stirring constantly, until eggs are set. Spoon eggs over muffins. Top with spaghetti sauce. Place ½ slice of cheese over sauce. Broil 3–4 minutes or until cheese melts. Makes 4 servings.

Grilled Ham Salad 'n' Cheese

An American favorite since way back when drugstores had lunch counters. This version from Miracle Whip Salad Dressing is special, very special indeed.

  2 cups finely chopped ham
⅓ cup Miracle Whip Salad Dressing
¼ cup sweet pickle relish
16 slices white bread
    Kraft Pure Prepared Mustard
16 Kraft American Singles Pasteurized Processed
    Cheese Food
    Soft Parkay Margarine

Combine meat, salad dressing and pickle relish; mix lightly. For each sandwich, spread two bread slices with mustard; cover one bread slice with one cheese food slice, ham mixture, second cheese food slice and second bread slice. Spread outside of sandwich with margarine; grill until lightly browned on both sides. Makes 8 sandwiches.

The California Club

It was 1933, Fred Astaire movies and bathtub gin martinis were "in" when Paul Evins, chef at a famous country club, invented the "club" sandwich. It's been a hit ever since and this version from the Avocado Growers is the best yet.

  4 avocados, sliced
  1 cup mayonnaise
¼ cup chili sauce
24 slices white toast
    Lettuce
  2 large tomatoes, sliced
  8 slices cooked turkey
  1 lb. bacon, cooked crisp
    Salt and pepper
    Pimiento-stuffed olives

Blend mayonnaise and chili sauce; spread on toast. Assemble 8 double-decker sandwiches with avocado and remaining ingredients. Add salt and pepper to taste. Quarter sandwiches; secure with cocktail picks and garnish with olives. Makes 8 sandwiches.

Open-Face Reubens

Corned beef on rye with Swiss cheese, onion rings, sauerkraut and a tangy dressing to top it all. Delicatessen fans, this is it!

Rye bread slices, toasted
Sauerkraut
Corned beef slices
Swiss cheese slices
Onion rings
Kraft Thousand Island
dressing

Cover toast with sauerkraut, meat, cheese and onions. Serve open-style with dressing.

Coney Islands

Get your Coney Island Red Hots! Get your red hots here! Campbell soup takes you back to Nathan's Pier restaurant on Coney Island in New York when hot dogs topped with spicy sauce and chopped onions went for ten cents each or three for a quarter.

4 frankfurters, split lengthwise
1 Tbs. butter or margarine
1 can Campbell's Chili Beef Soup
⅓ cup water
4 frankfurter buns, split and toasted
  Chopped onion

In skillet, brown frankfurters in butter. Add soup, water. Heat; stir. Place frankfurters in buns; spoon chili over. Garnish with onion. Makes 4 sandwiches.

Spring Salad Sandwich

Make this meatless creation from Lea & Perrins for a gourmet vegetarian or for anyone who enjoys a great sandwich.

1 8-oz. package cream cheese, softened
¼ cup dairy sour cream
¼ cup chopped celery
¼ cup grated carrot
2 Tbs. chopped radishes
2 Tbs. minced scallions
1 tsp. Lea & Perrins Worcestershire Sauce
8 slices pumpernickel bread

In a small bowl thoroughly combine cream cheese, sour cream, celery, carrot, radishes, scallions and Lea & Perrins. Spread a heaping ⅓ cup on each of 4 slices of bread. Top with remaining bread and cut in half. Makes 4 sandwiches.

Sausage en Croute

Here's a "sandwich" that's just made to star at your next brunch party. Created by Pepperidge Farm when they introduced their new Frozen Puff Pastry Sheets.

1 sheet Pepperidge Farm Frozen "Bake It Fresh"
    Puff Pastry
1 lb. pork sausage
½ cup chopped onion
⅓ cup chopped green pepper
1 large tomato, diced
1 cup shredded Swiss cheese
3 Tbs. chopped parsley

Thaw puff pastry sheet 20 minutes. Meanwhile, in a skillet, brown sausage stirring to break into bits. Add onion and green pepper and cook until tender. Remove from heat and pour off drippings. Add tomato, cheese and parsley. Unfold and roll out pastry on lightly floured board to 14 × 10-inch rectangle. Transfer to baking sheet lined with brown paper. Spread sausage mixture on pastry. Roll up from long side jelly roll fashion. Pinch edges to seal. Form into circle, pinch together. Cut ⅔ way through roll at 1½ inch intervals and turn pieces up with cut side showing. Bake at 425°F. for 20 minutes or until golden. Makes 6–8 servings.

Egg Salad Filling

"Can you give me a recipe for a really tasty egg salad filling?" Requests like this were so frequent at the French's Mustard test kitchens that they developed this recipe. It's just the right amount of mustard plus the celery salt that turns the trick.

4 hard-cooked eggs, finely chopped
¼ cup finely chopped celery
1 Tbs. French's Prepared Mustard
2 Tbs. mayonnaise

1 Tbs. parsley flakes
¼ tsp. celery salt
1 tsp. sugar

Combine ingredients and mix thoroughly. Makes enough filling for 4–6 sandwiches.

Peanut Butter 'n' Bacon Sandwich

Not for the kindergarten crowd; Lea & Perrins developed this peanut butter sandwich for gourmets.

¼ cup peanut butter
2 strips crisp bacon, crumbled
2 tsps. Lea & Perrins Worcestershire Sauce
2 tsps. instant minced onion
2 slices bread

Combine all ingredients. Spread on slice of bread. Top with second slice. Makes 1 sandwich.

7.
Breads:
Yeast Breads,
Quick Breads,
Rolls and Muffins

When a friend opened her house for guests recently, she put a loaf of homemade bread in the oven just before the stream of visitors began to arrive. Her house is pretty, but that aroma of freshly baked bread transformed it into a home with all the warmth and charm that means. This is not to say you should bake your own bread just for fragrance, but it's a fact that nothing smells quite so good or tastes quite so great as freshly baked bread, and nothing else spells home in quite the same delicious way.

However, all the romantic prose in the world will not improve a heavy, tasteless loaf or a dry and crumbly muffin. It's all very well to carry on about the joy of homemade breads, but the price of ingredients being what they are, few cooks can afford failures and, until recently, homemade bread was a "chancy" thing. No longer. The "guess" has been taken out of bread-making by the flour millers, the yeast makers, and producers of shortening and grains—in fact, all the companies who employ the best cooks in the business to perfect bread, muffins, rolls and biscuits that are a joy to make as well as to eat.

I've made sure especially to include all those lovely "special" breads; old-fashioned gingerbread, Swedish tea ring, oatmeal muffins, a hearty whole wheat loaf and, of course, that all-time most-requested recipe, baking powder biscuits. There are yeast breads and quick breads, new-method breads that are double quick to make. Every one is easy, in fact, fail proof. Our test-kitchen experts have seen to that.

Ralston Whole Wheat Bread

When I first tasted this bread, it seemed the very essence of wheat, it tasted of wheat, smelled of wheat and the crust was the color of ripe wheat. Requests for this recipe from the Ralston® Purina Company have increased over the years.

2¼ cups Instant or Regular Ralston® Cereal
¼ cup sugar
1 Tbs. salt
⅓ cup vegetable shortening
4 cups (1 quart) milk, scalded
2 packages active dry yeast
½ cup warm water
7–8 cups all-purpose flour

Grease three 8½ × 4½ × 2½-inch loaf pans. Combine Ralston, sugar, salt and shortening in large bowl. Add hot, scalded milk. Stir until thoroughly moistened. Cool to warm (105°–115°), stirring occasionally. Dissolve yeast in water. Stir into cereal mixture. Add 2 cups flour. Mix well. Gradually stir in enough additional flour to form a stiff dough. Place on floured surface. Knead until smooth and elastic (8–10 minutes). Work in additional flour as needed. Form into ball. Place in greased bowl. Turn to grease all sides. Cover. Let rise in warm place, free from draft, until double in bulk (about 1 hour).

Punch down dough. Place on lightly floured surface. Knead about 2 minutes. Divide dough in thirds. Form into loaves. Place in pans. Cover. Let rise in warm place until almost double in bulk (about 30 minutes). Bake in pre-heated 400°F. oven about 30 minutes or until browned and bread sounds hollow when lightly tapped. Remove from pans at once. Cool on rack. Makes 3 loaves.
Note: For golden brown, shiny top, brush tops with beaten egg before baking.

Sixty-Minute Rolls

Hot from the oven freshly made rolls for Sunday brunch, or any night supper. A rapid mix recipe from the Fleischmann's Yeast package. You'll love it.

3½ to 4½ cups unsifted flour
3 Tbs. sugar
1 tsp. salt
2 packages Fleischmann's Active Dry Yeast
1 cup milk
½ cup water
¼ cup (½ stick) Fleischmann's Margarine

In a large bowl thoroughly mix 1½ cups flour, sugar, salt, and undissolved Fleischmann's Active Dry Yeast. Combine milk, water and Fleischmann's Margarine in a saucepan. Heat over low heat until liquids are very warm (120–130°F.). Margarine does not need to melt. Gradually add to dry ingredients and beat 2 minutes at medium speed of electric mixer, scraping bowl occasionally. Add ½ cup flour. Beat at high speed 2 minutes, scraping bowl occasionally. Stir in enough additional flour to make a soft dough. Turn out onto lightly floured board; knead until smooth and elastic, about 5 minutes. Place in greased bowl, turning dough to grease top. Cover; place bowl in pan of water of about 98°F. Let rise 15 minutes. Turn dough out onto floured board. Divide in half and shape as Curlicues or Lucky Clovers (below). Cover; let rise in warm place, free from draft (about 90°F.), 15 minutes. Bake at 425°F. about 12 minutes, or until done. Remove from baking sheets and cool on wire racks.

Variations:

Curlicues: Roll out each half to a 12 × 9-inch rectangle. Cut into 12 equal strips (about 1-inch wide). Hold one end of strip firmly and wind closely to form coil. Tuck end firmly underneath. Place on greased baking sheets about 2 inches apart.

Lucky Clovers: Form each half into a 12-inch roll. Cut into 12 equal pieces. Form into balls; place in greased muffin pans 2¾ × 1¼ inches. With scissors, cut each ball in half, then into quarters, cutting through almost to bottom of rolls.

Frozen Dinner Rolls

Here's the very first recipe from Fleischmann's Yeast Company for your own freeze now, bake later, rolls. It's still one of their most popular.

5½ to 6½ cups unsifted flour
 ½ cup sugar
1½ tsps. salt
 2 packages Fleischmann's Active Dry Yeast

1¼ cups water
½ cup milk
⅓ cup Fleischmann's Margarine
2 eggs (at room temperature)

In a large bowl thoroughly mix 2 cups flour, sugar, salt, and undissolved Fleischmann's Active Dry Yeast.

Combine water, milk and Fleischmann's Margarine in a saucepan. Heat over low heat until liquids are very warm (120– 130°F.). Margarine does not need to melt. Gradually add to dry ingredients and beat 2 minutes at medium speed of electric mixer, scraping bowl occasionally. Add eggs and ½ cup flour. Beat at high speed 2 minutes, scraping bowl occasionally. Stir in enough additional flour to make a soft dough. Turn out onto lightly floured board; knead until smooth and elastic, about 8– 10 minutes. Cover with plastic wrap, then a towel, let rest 20 minutes.

Punch dough down. Shape into desired shapes for dinner rolls. Place on greased baking sheets.* Cover with plastic wrap and foil, sealing well. Freeze until firm. Transfer to plastic bags. Freeze up to 4 weeks.

Remove from freezer; place on greased baking sheets. Cover; let rise in warm place, free from draft, until doubled in bulk, about 1½ hours. Bake at 350°F. 15 minutes, or until golden brown and done. Remove from baking sheets and cool on wire racks.

* Editor's note: These can be baked immediately, if desired.

Sally Lunn

The lovely thing about this old-fashioned favorite from the Fleischmann Yeast package is that no kneading is required.

½ cup warm water (105–115°F.)
1 package Fleischmann's Active Dry Yeast
1 cup warm milk
½ cup (1 stick) softened Fleischmann's Margarine
¼ cup sugar
2 tsps. salt
3 eggs, well beaten (at room temperature)
5½–6 cups unsifted flour

Measure warm water into large warm bowl. Sprinkle in Fleischmann's Yeast; stir until dissolved. Add milk, Fleischmann's Margarine, sugar, salt and eggs. Stir in 3 cups flour. Beat until well-blended, about 1 minute. Stir in enough remaining flour to make a soft dough. Cover; let rise in warm place, free from draft, until doubled in bulk, about 1 hour.

Stir down; spoon into well-greased and floured 10-inch tube pan or 2 well-greased 9 × 5 × 3-inch loaf pans. Cover; let rise in warm place, free from draft, until doubled in bulk, about 1 hour.

Bake large loaf at 400°F. about 30 minutes, or until done. Bake small loaves at 375°F. about 30 minutes, or until done. Remove from pans and cool on wire racks.

Baking Powder Biscuits

This is the "remembered" Crisco recipe that's been used by over three generations of good cooks who "don't need a recipe to knock out a few biscuits for goodness' sake!"

2 cups sifted flour
3 tsps. baking powder
1 tsp. salt
⅓ cup Crisco
¾ cup milk

Preheat oven to 425°F. In bowl, combine the flour, baking powder and salt. Cut in Crisco until mixture resembles coarse meal. Add milk; stir with fork until blended. Transfer dough to a lightly floured surface. Knead gently, 8–10 times. Roll dough ½ inch thick. Cut with floured cutter. Bake on ungreased baking sheet at 425°F. for 12–15 minutes. Makes 12–16 biscuits.

Homemade Crisco Quick Bread Mix

And here's that "most asked for" quick bread mix from Crisco. (See following recipe also.)

10 cups sifted flour
⅓ cup baking powder
¼ cup sugar
1 Tbs. salt
2 cups Crisco

In large bowl, combine the flour, baking powder, sugar and salt. Cut Crisco into dry ingredients with pastry blender till mixture resembles coarse meal. Store in covered container up to 6 weeks at room temperature. For longer storage, place in freezer. To measure, spoon mix into measuring cup; level with spatula. Makes 12 cups.

Quick Mix Biscuits

2 cups Homemade Crisco Quick Bread Mix
½ cup milk

Preheat oven to 425°F. In bowl, make a well in the Crisco
Quick Bread Mix; add milk all at once. Stir quickly with
fork just till blended. Transfer dough to a lightly floured
surface. Knead gently 8–10 times. Roll dough ½–¾ inch
thick. Cut with floured biscuit cutter. Bake on ungreased
baking sheet at 425°F. about 12–15 minutes. Makes 8–10
biscuits.

Giant Popovers

**The Planters Peanut Company tells me they receive steady
requests for this recipe and have for years.**

6 eggs
¼ cup Planters Peanut Oil
2 cups milk
1¾ cups unsifted flour
1½ tsps. salt

In large bowl, combine eggs and Planters Peanut Oil;
beat slightly. Gradually beat in milk, flour and salt. Pour
batter into 10 well-oiled custard cups. Place custard cups
on baking sheet. Bake in moderate oven (375°F.) 1 hour,
or until firm and brown. If desired, remove popovers
from oven after 45 minutes, cut slit in the side of each to
let steam escape, quickly return to oven for last 15 minutes. Makes 10 large popovers.

Pioneer Corn Bread

This authentic, old-timey corn bread from Elam's is the best you'll ever bake. Served with corn syrup and lots of melty soft butter, it's a treat you'll long remember.

2 cups Elam's Stone Ground Yellow Corn Meal
2 tsps. baking powder
1 tsp. soda
1 tsp. salt
1 egg, beaten slightly
1 cup buttermilk
¼ cup cooking oil or melted shortening

Combine first four ingredients in bowl; mix well. Add buttermilk, egg and oil or melted shortening. Stir just until dry ingredients are moistened; do not beat. Pour into well-greased 8-inch square baking pan dusted with Elam's Yellow Corn Meal. Bake in hot oven (425°F.) 20 minutes or until done and a light golden brown. Makes 16 pieces, 2 inches square.

Variations: Follow recipe for Pioneer Corn Bread above and change as suggested below:

Sweet Milk Corn Bread: Substitute sweet milk for buttermilk. Increase baking powder to 3 tsps. and omit soda.

Muffins: Fill well-greased medium size muffin cups ⅔ full. Reduce baking time to 12–15 minutes or until done and a light golden brown. Makes 12 2½ × 1⅛-inch muffins.

Oatmeal Muffins

Your mother may have made these muffins; if so you'll remember how good they tasted, hot from the oven, lavish with sweet butter and homemade jam.

  3 cups Elam's Scotch Style Oatmeal
  3 Tbs. sugar
  3 tsps. baking powder
  ¾ tsp. salt
1½ cups milk
  1 egg, beaten
  3 Tbs. cooking oil or melted shortening

Combine first 4 ingredients in bowl; mix. Combine milk, egg and oil or melted shortening; beat slightly. Add liquids to dry ingredients; stir just until dry ingredients are moistened. Fill greased muffin cups (2½ × 1¼ inches) about ⅞ full using an equal amount of batter in each cup. Bake in hot oven (425°F.) until done and lightly browned, 20–25 minutes. Makes 12 muffins.

Two-Hour Nut Roll

Super great tasting but super quick to make. This beautiful coffee cake with its old world flavor was one of the first new rapid-mix method recipes from Fleischmann's Yeast.

6–7 cups unsifted flour
  3 Tbs. sugar
  1 tsp. salt
  2 packages Fleischmann's Active Dry Yeast
  1 cup dairy sour cream
  ½ cup water
  1 cup (2 sticks) Fleischmann's Margarine
  3 eggs (at room temperature)

In a large bowl thoroughly mix 2 cups flour, sugar, salt and dissolved Fleischmann's Active Dry Yeast. Combine sour cream, water and Fleischmann's Margarine in a saucepan. Heat over low heat until liquids are very warm (120– 130°F.). Margarine does not need to melt. Gradually add to dry ingredients and beat 2 minutes at medium speed of electric mixer, scraping bowl occasionally. Add eggs and 1 cup flour. Beat at high speed 2 minutes, scraping bowl occasionally. Stir in enough additional flour to make a soft dough. Turn out onto lightly floured board; knead a few times to form a ball. Cover and let rest 10 minutes.

Divide dough into 4 equal pieces. Roll out each piece into a 14 × 12-inch rectangle. Spread each with one-fourth of either of the nut fillings (below). Roll each up from long side, as for jelly roll. Seal edges. Place on greased baking sheets, sealed edges down. Cover; let rise in warm place, free from draft, until doubled in bulk, about 1 hour. Bake at 350°F. about 35 minutes, or until done. Remove from baking sheets and cool on wire racks. When cool, if desired, drizzle with confectioners' sugar frosting.

Maple Walnut Filling: Melt ¾ cup (1½ sticks) Fleischmann's Margarine over low heat. Stir in ½ cup sugar and 3 Tbs. imitation maple flavor. Add 5 cups ground Planters or Southern Belle English Walnuts; blend well.

Pecan Filling: Melt 1 cup (2 sticks) Fleischmann's Margarine over low heat. Stir in ½ cup sugar and ¼ cup vanilla extract. Add 7 cups (4 6-oz. cans) ground Planters or Southern Belle Pecans; blend well.

Editor's note: These freeze well if you can't eat them all at once.

Swedish Tea Ring

Around Christmas time this is the most requested recipe at the Parkay Margarine test kitchens. It's just perfect for Christmas morning breakfast.

2½–3 cups flour
 ¼ cup sugar
 1 pkg. active dry yeast
 1 tsp. salt
 ½ cup milk
 ¼ cup water
   Parkay margarine
 1 egg

¼ cup Parkay Margarine, melted
½ cup raisins
¼ cup granulated sugar
¼ cup packed brown sugar
¼ cup chopped nuts
1 tsp. cinnamon
Vanilla Drizzle (below)

In large mixing bowl, combine 1 cup flour, sugar, yeast and salt. Heat milk, water and ⅓ cup margarine over low heat until warm. Add to flour mixture; beat 3 minutes at medium speed of electric mixer. Add ½ cup flour and egg; beat 2 minutes at high speed. Stir in enough remaining flour to form a soft dough. On lightly floured surface, knead dough until smooth and elastic. Place in greased bowl; brush with melted margarine. Cover; let rise in warm place until double in volume, about 1½ hours. Punch down dough; let rest 10 minutes.

On lightly floured surface, roll out dough to 15 × 10-inch rectangle. Brush with margarine; sprinkle with combined raisins, sugars, nuts and cinnamon. Roll up, starting at long end; seal long end. Place on greased cookie sheet. Join ends to form ring; seal ends. With scissors, cut two-thirds of the way through ring at 1-inch intervals; turn each section on its side. Let rise until double in volume, about 45 minutes. Bake at 350°F., 25–30 minutes. Drizzle with Vanilla Drizzle.

Vanilla Drizzle

1 cup sifted confectioners' sugar
1 Tbs. milk
1 tsp. vanilla

Combine ingredients; mix well.

Orange Juice Muffins with Honey Spread

These muffins were always called Adele's favorite in our house. If you had the recipe but lost it, for goodness sake, don't lose it again.

2 cups Bisquick® Baking
   Mix
2 Tbs. sugar
1 egg
1 tsp. grated orange peel
⅔ cup orange juice

2 Tbs. sugar
¼ tsp. ground cinnamon
⅛ tsp. ground nutmeg
   Honey Spread (below)

Heat oven to 400°F. Grease bottoms only of 12 medium muffin cups. Mix baking mix, 2 Tbs. sugar, the egg, orange peel and orange juice; beat vigorously 30 seconds. Fill muffin cups about ⅔ full. Mix 2 Tbs. sugar, the cinnamon and nutmeg. Sprinkle each muffin with about ½ tsp. sugar mixture. Bake 15 minutes. Serve with Honey Spread. 12 muffins.

Honey Spread: Beat ½ cup margarine or butter, softened, and ½ cup honey until fluffy.

Raisin Muffins

Old-fashioned muffins with a "down-home" taste. From the Ralston Purina® Company's Checkerboard Kitchens.

1 egg, slightly beaten
1 cup milk
3 Tbs. vegetable oil
⅓ cup raisins
1¾ cups Bran Chex® cereal
1 cup sifted all-purpose flour
⅓ cup sugar
2 tsps. baking powder
½ tsp. salt
½ tsp. cinnamon

Preheat oven to 400°F. Grease twelve (2½-inch) muffin cups. Combine egg, milk, oil, raisins and Bran Chex®. Let stand 10 minutes. Meanwhile, sift together dry ingredients. Stir Bran Chex® cereal mixture to blend. Add all at once to dry ingredients. Stir only until moistened. Fill muffin cups ⅔ full. Bake 20 minutes or until lightly browned. Makes 12 muffins.

Blueberry Muffins

An old-fashioned, not-too-sweet berry muffin, from the Parkay Margarine test kitchens. Just try them, still warm from the oven, with steaming hot mugs of freshly made coffee.

2 cups flour
⅓ cup sugar
2 tsps. baking powder
½ tsp. salt
1 egg, slightly beaten

¾ cup milk
½ cup Parkay Margarine, melted
1 cup fresh blueberries

Combine dry ingredients. Add combined egg, milk and margarine, mixing just until moistened. Fold in blueberries. Spoon into greased and floured medium-size muffin pan, filling each cup ⅔ full. Bake at 425°F., 20–25 minutes or until golden brown. Makes 1 dozen muffins.

Variations: Substitute for fresh blueberries 1 cup:
Well-drained, thawed frozen blueberries or cranberries
Well-drained pitted dark sweet cherries
Fresh cranberries

Harvest Tea Loaf

Bake this, set out the creamy butter, brew a pot of tea and ask your mother-in-law over—it's that good. A surprise recipe from Gerber Baby Foods.

¾ cup sugar
⅓ cup shortening
2 eggs
1 7½-oz. jar Junior Gerber Squash
1½ cups sifted all-purpose flour
½ tsp. baking powder
1 tsp. soda
¾ tsp. salt
½ tsp. cinnamon
½ tsp. cloves
⅓ cup chopped nuts
⅓ cup chopped dates

Cream shortening and sugar until light and fluffy. Add eggs, one at a time, beating well after each addition. Add squash. Sift together flour, baking powder, soda, salt and spices. Reserve ¼ cup flour mixture and work it into the dates and nuts. Add flour mixture to squash mixture. Stir dates and nuts into batter. Turn batter into greased 9 × 5 × 3½-inch pan. Bake at 350°F. for about 1 hour or until done. Makes 1 loaf.

Apple Spice Coffee Cake

This is a long-time favorite from Parkay Margarine, so good it deserves company. A fall time, crisp apple time, coffee klatsch perhaps? Be sure to serve with plenty of coffee.

½ cup Parkay Margarine
1 cup granulated sugar
¾ cup packed brown sugar
2 eggs
1 tsp. vanilla
3 cups flour
1 Tbs. baking powder

1 tsp. salt
1 tsp. ground allspice
1 tsp. ground cloves
1 cup milk
3 cups peeled apple slices
1 tsp. cinnamon

Cream margarine, ¾ cup granulated sugar and brown sugar until light and fluffy. Blend in eggs and vanilla. Add combined flour, baking powder, salt, allspice and cloves alternately with milk; mix well after each addition. Pour into greased 13 × 9-inch baking pan. Arrange apples on batter; sprinkle with combined ¼ cup granulated sugar and cinnamon. Bake at 375°F., 40–45 minutes or until wooden pick inserted in center comes out clean.

Quick Nut Bread

There's something very satisfying about this whole wheat sweet bread from Elam's. It's nothing sensational, but it's the kind of thing people ask if you've made lately when they drop in for a cup of coffee or tea.

3 cups Elam's Stone Ground 100% Whole
  Wheat Flour
4 tsps. baking powder
1 tsp. salt
½ cup soft shortening

1 cup sugar
3 eggs
2 tsps. vanilla
1¼ cups milk
1 cup finely chopped walnuts or pecans

Combine first 3 ingredients in bowl; mix well and reserve. Cream shortening; add sugar gradually beating well after each addition. Add eggs, one at a time, beating well after each addition. Stir in vanilla and milk; mix until smooth. Add dry ingredients, ¼ at a time, blending well after each addition. Fold in chopped nuts. Spoon into greased loaf pan (9 × 5 × 3-inch). Bake in moderate oven (350°F.) until done, 60–70 minutes. Cool in pan 10 minutes; loosen edges and remove bread from pan. Finish cooling on wire rack. Makes one loaf.

Old-Fashioned Date and Nut Bread

Here's the all time best American style recipe from the Dromedary Date people. I like it served with a bowl of cream cheese whipped up with a bit of sour cream and cups of fragrant freshly made coffee.

¾ cup water
¼ cup shortening
1 8-oz. package Dromedary Chopped Dates or Dromedary Pitted Dates, snipped.

¾ cup chopped walnuts
2 eggs, slightly beaten
½ tsp. vanilla extract
1½ cups all-purpose flour
¾ cup granulated sugar
1½ tsps. baking soda
½ tsp. salt

Preheat oven to 350°F. Grease and flour a 9 × 5 × 3-inch loaf pan. In small saucepan, bring water and shortening to a boil; pour over dates in a medium bowl. Allow mixture to stand 15 minutes. Stir to blend. Add nuts, eggs and vanilla. In small bowl, combine flour, sugar, baking soda and salt. Stir into date mixture until blended. Do not overmix. Pour into pan. Bake 65–70 minutes or until cake tester inserted in center comes out clean. Cool in pan on wire rack 10 minutes. Loosen edges with spatula; turn out on wire rack to cool completely. Makes 1 loaf.

Crescent Caramel Swirl

Birth of a new classic. This recipe won the $25,000 Grand Prize at the 27th Pillsbury Bake-Off® Contest in 1976.

½ cup margarine or butter
½ cup chopped nuts
1 cup firmly packed brown sugar
2 Tbs. water
2 8-oz. cans Pillsbury Refrigerated Quick
  Crescent Dinner Rolls

Heat oven to 375°F. (350°F. for colored fluted tube pan.) In small saucepan, melt margarine. Coat bottom and sides of 12-cup fluted tube pan (do not use pan with removable bottom) with 2 Tbs. of the melted margarine; sprinkle pan with 3 Tbs. of the nuts. Add remaining nuts, brown sugar and water to margarine; heat to boiling, stirring occasionally. Remove dough from cans in rolled sections; do not unroll. Cut each section into 4 slices. Arrange 8 slices in prepared pan, separating each pinwheel slightly to allow sauce to penetrate. Spoon half the caramel sauce over dough. Repeat with remaining dough, topping slices in pan; pour remaining caramel sauce over dough.

Bake at 375°F. for 25–30 minutes (30–35 minutes for colored fluted tube pan) or until deep golden brown. Cool 3 minutes; turn onto serving platter or waxed paper. Makes 1 coffee cake ring.

Grandmother's Delicious Gingerbread

An old-fashioned favorite cake-like gingerbread, from the Crisco test kitchens. The recipe was developed almost 20 years ago but it's still in demand.

1 cup brown sugar
½ cup Crisco
2 eggs
¾ cup molasses
2¾ cups sifted regular flour
2 tsps. soda

2 tsps. ginger
1 tsp. cinnamon
½ tsp. salt
1 cup buttermilk or sour milk*
Ice cream, whipped cream or applesauce

Blend sugar, Crisco and eggs. Stir in molasses. Add combined dry ingredients alternately with buttermilk; beat well. Spread in a well-greased and floured 13 × 9 × 2-inch pan. Bake at 350°F. for 35–40 minutes. Serve warm with ice cream, whipped cream or applesauce.

* To sour milk, add 1 Tbs. vinegar to 1 cup milk.

Sugar-Coated Sour Milk Doughnuts

One of my friends in Maine has the distinction of frying the best doughnuts in the entire state. Her secret? Here's what she says, "It's not just the recipe, though that must be good, but it's the way you fry them too. I use Crisco and the recipe

from the can but it's my 'knack' that really makes them so good." (See below).

4 cups sifted flour
1 tsp. baking soda
1 tsp. salt
1 tsp. ground nutmeg
½ tsp. cream of tartar
¾ cup sugar
¼ cup Crisco
3 eggs
1 cup sour milk (1 Tbs. vinegar plus enough milk
   to make 1 cup)
   Crisco for deep frying

Combine the flour, baking soda, salt, nutmeg, and cream of tartar. In large mixing bowl, cream the ¾ cup sugar and the Crisco; beat in eggs. Add flour mixture alternately with sour milk, beating just till blended. Cover and chill at least 2 hours. On floured surface, roll dough ⅜ inch thick. Cut with floured 2½-inch doughnut cutter. Fry in deep Crisco heated to 365°F. till doughnuts are golden brown, about 2–3 minutes, turning once. Drain on paper toweling. Roll in granulated sugar. Makes 24 doughnuts and 24 holes.

My Friend's "knack" tips:

On lightly floured surface, roll chilled dough about ¼ inch thick. Dip doughnut cutter in flour between cuts; cut straight down.

Heat Crisco in saucepan to 365°F. using frying thermometer to check temperature. Fry a few doughnuts at a time, turning once.

Use a slotted spoon or fork to remove doughnuts from hot Crisco. Drain on paper toweling before frosting or sugar coating.

8.
Favorite
Pies
and Cakes

There's an old expression, "As American as apple pie," and we do all love pies. Was there ever anything as good as a perfect apple pie? I think not, unless it was a towering layer cake regal in its robe of icing and in its own way just as all American as pie. Or maybe an old-fashioned upside-down cake, its caramely sweetness glazing perfect rounds of pineapple or peaches. Then there are the loaf cakes spiced with raisins and nuts, an American tradition in its own right. For that matter what could be more American than Chocolate Meringue Pie? Deep, dark and delicious under an airy cloud of meringue.

More sophisticated desserts may come and go, fashion and fads being what they are, but our fondness for the incomparable deliciousness of homemade pies and cakes never changes.

The cakes and pies included here are the ones our food companies find to be most asked for year in and year out.

So here they are, the sure-fire, can't-fail, recipes for your best beloved cakes and pies. Some new favorites are included too, each one destined to make any meal an event. Think about it. Did you ever see anyone look unhappy when you brought out a really gorgeous cake or pie?

And gorgeous they will be, from the dazzling richness of Black Forest Layer Cake to the silky lightness of Pumpkin Chiffon pie—each is perfection in its own right.

Bavarian Apple Torte

Kraft tells me this *is* a Bavarian torte, but I do believe it is a first cousin to the Pennsylvania Dutch apple torte. Well no matter, I'm not one to quarrel with ancestry when the results are this good.

½ cup Parkay Margarine
⅓ cup sugar
¼ tsp. vanilla
1 cup flour
1 8-oz. package Philadelphia Brand Cream Cheese
¼ cup sugar
1 egg
½ tsp. vanilla
4 cups thin peeled apple slices
⅓ cup sugar
½ tsp. cinnamon
¼ cup sliced almonds

Cream margarine and sugar until light and fluffy. Blend in vanilla. Add flour; mix well. Spread on bottom and sides of 9-inch springform pan. Combine softened cream cheese and sugar, mixing until well blended. Blend in egg and vanilla. Pour into pastry-lined pan. Toss apples with combined sugar and cinnamon; spoon over cream cheese layer. Sprinkle with nuts. Bake at 450°F., 10 minutes. Reduce oven temperature to 400°F.; continue baking 25 minutes. Loosen crust from rim of pan; cool before removing rim of pan. Makes 8– 10 servings.

Hunt's Very Special Spice Cake

An all-time favorite from Hunt's Tomato Sauce label. This cake stays marvelously moist for days.

3 cups sifted flour
1½ cups sugar
1½ tsp. baking powder
1½ tsp. cinnamon
¾ tsp. nutmeg
¾ tsp. cloves
¾ tsp. allspice
¾ tsp. salt

1 8-oz. can Hunt's Tomato Sauce
1½ tsp. baking soda
2 eggs, beaten
¾ cup pure vegetable oil
1 cup chopped nuts
1½ cup golden raisins
½ cup orange or pineapple juice

In large mixing bowl, combine flour, sugar, baking powder, spices and salt. Thoroughly mix Hunt's Tomato Sauce and soda in small bowl; add to flour mixture. Stir in eggs, oil, nuts, raisins and fruit juice; mix well. Pour into greased 10-inch Bundt or tube pan. Bake at 350°F. 45–55 minutes. Cool in pan 15 minutes before turning out on serving plate. Dust top with powdered sugar. Makes one 10-inch cake.

Grandma's Upside-Down Cake

I'm told that Fannie Farmer made this cake famous. In her day it was a sensation. It still is, thanks to this excellent recipe from the Dole test kitchens.

1 1 lb., 4 oz. can Dole Sliced Pineapple
¼ cup butter
⅔ cup brown sugar, firmly packed
   Maraschino cherries
1 cup flour
¾ cup sugar
1½ tsp. baking powder
½ tsp. salt

½ cup milk
¼ cup shortening
1 egg
1 tsp. lemon juice
1 tsp. vanilla
¼ tsp. grated lemon peel

Drain pineapple, reserving 2 Tbs. syrup. Melt butter in a 10-inch cast iron skillet.* Stir in brown sugar until blended. Remove from heat. Arrange pineapple slices in sugar mixture. Place a Maraschino cherry in center of each slice. Combine flour, sugar, baking powder and salt. Add milk and shortening; beat 2 minutes. Add egg, reserved syrup, lemon juice, vanilla and lemon peel; beat 2 minutes. Pour over pineapple in skillet, spreading evenly. Bake in a 350°F. oven 40 minutes. Cool on wire rack 5 minutes. Invert onto serving plate. Serve warm. Makes 8 servings.

* If using a skillet with wooden handle, wrap well with foil.

Hollywood Cheesecake

This is the famous Philadelphia Brand Cream Cheese cheesecake recipe that made cheesecake popular in the 1940's, not just in California and New York, but across the country. As most good cooks know, you can top it with anything from fresh strawberries to canned (drained) cherries, pineapple or raspberry jam—and so on and so on.

1 cup graham cracker
  crumbs
3 Tbs. sugar
3 Tbs. margarine, melted
2 8-oz. packages
  Philadelphia Brand
  Cream Cheese

½ cup sugar
1 Tbs. lemon juice
1 tsp. grated lemon rind
½ tsp. vanilla
2 eggs, separated
1 cup dairy sour cream
2 Tbs. sugar
1 tsp. vanilla

Combine crumbs, sugar and margarine, press onto bottom of 9-inch springform pan. Bake at 325°F., 10 minutes. Combine softened cream cheese, sugar, lemon juice, rind and vanilla, mixing at medium speed on electric mixer until well blended. Add egg yolks, one at a time, mixing well after each addition. Fold in stiffly beaten egg whites; pour over crust. Bake at 300°F., 45 minutes. Combine sour cream, sugar and vanilla. Carefully spread over cheesecake; continue baking 10 minutes. Loosen cake rim of pan; cool before removing rim of pan. Chill.

Black Forest Cake

There are days when I just long to get out to the kitchen and create something really special and this is certainly the recipe for those times. High, wide and handsome, it's a spectacular from Parkay Margarine.

1¼ cups sugar
⅔ cup Squeeze Parkay Margarine
3 eggs
3 1-oz. squares unsweetened chocolate, melted

1 tsp. vanilla
1¾ cups flour
1 tsp. baking powder
1 tsp. baking soda
1 tsp. salt
⅔ cup buttermilk
Chocolate Filling (below)
Brandied Cherry Filling (below)
Whipped Cream Frosting (below)

Combine sugar and margarine. Add eggs, one at a time, mixing well after each addition. Blend in chocolate and vanilla. Add combined dry ingredients alternately with buttermilk, mixing well after each addition. Pour into two greased and floured 8-inch layer pans. Bake at 350°F., 30–35 minutes or until wooden pick inserted in center comes out clean. Cool 10 minutes; remove from pans. Cool; split each layer in half horizontally. Spread one layer with Chocolate Filling; top with second layer spread with Brandied Cherry Filling. Repeat with remaining layers. Frost sides with Whipped Cream Frosting.

Chocolate Filling

1 cup heavy cream
¼ cup confectioners' sugar
1 Tbs. cocoa
½ tsp. vanilla

Beat cream until slightly thickened; gradually add sugar, cocoa and vanilla, beating until stiff peaks form.

Brandied Cherry Filling

1 16-oz. can pitted sour cherries or
1 16-oz. package frozen sour cherries, thawed
2 Tbs. cornstarch
¼ cup sugar
2 Tbs. brandy

Drain cherries, reserving ¾ cup syrup. Combine cornstarch and sugar in saucepan; gradually add reserved syrup. Cook over medium heat until mixture is clear and thickened. Stir in cherries and brandy. Cool.

Whipped Cream Frosting

1 cup heavy cream
¼ cup confectioners' sugar
½ tsp. vanilla

Beat cream until slightly thickened; gradually add sugar and vanilla, beating until stiff peaks form.

Sour Cream Chocolate Cake

A half-century of good cooks have baked this Chocolate Sour Cream Cake. It's as moist, rich and delicious as it was when it was first printed on the back of Hershey's Baking Chocolate package some 20 years ago.

 3 blocks (3 oz.) Hershey's Baking Chocolate
½ cup butter or margarine
 1 cup boiling water
 2 cups light brown sugar, packed
 2 cups all-purpose flour
1½ tsps. baking soda
 1 tsp. salt
 2 eggs
½ cup dairy sour cream
 1 tsp. vanilla
   Sour Cream Filling and Icing (see recipe below)

Combine baking chocolate, butter or margarine and boiling water in a small bowl; stir until chocolate and butter or margarine are melted. Thoroughly combine brown sugar, flour, baking soda and salt in a large mixer bowl. Gradually add chocolate mixture, beating until thoroughly combined. Blend in eggs, sour cream and vanilla; beat one minute at medium speed. Pour into a greased and floured 13 × 9 × 2-inch pan. Bake at 350°F. for 35– 40 minutes. Cool and frost.

Chocolate Sour Cream Filling and Icing

2 cups granulated sugar
6 Tbs. Hershey's Chocolate Flavored Syrup
⅔ cup sour cream (dairy)
1 tsp. vanilla

In a saucepan, combine the sugar and chocolate syrup. When well mixed, add the sour cream, and cook over medium heat to the soft-ball stage (234°F.). Remove from the fire; add vanilla and beat until thick enough to spread. Add nuts of any kind for variety. Yields 1½ cups icing.

Sweet Chocolate Cake

A truly memorable classic from Baker's Chocolate.

1 4-oz. package Baker's German's Sweet
  Chocolate
½ cup boiling water
1 cup butter or margarine
2 cups sugar
4 egg yolks
1 tsp. vanilla
2½ cups sifted cake flour
1 tsp. soda
½ tsp. salt
1 cup buttermilk
4 egg whites, stiffly beaten
  Coconut-Pecan Frosting (below)

Melt chocolate in boiling water. Cool. Cream butter and sugar until light and fluffy. Add egg yolks, one at a time, beating after each addition. Add vanilla and melted chocolate; mix until blended. Measure sifted flour, soda, and salt and sift together. Then add flour mixture and buttermilk alternately to chocolate mixture, beating after each addition until batter is smooth. Fold in egg whites. Pour batter into three 8- or 9-inch layer pans, lined on bottoms with paper. Bake in moderate oven (350°F.) for 35–40 minutes for 8-inch layers or 30–35 minutes for 9-inch layers. Cool. (This delicate cake will have a flat contour and a slightly sugary top crust which tends to crack.) Frost top and between layers with Coconut-Pecan Frosting.

Coconut-Pecan Frosting

A heavenly icing just made for Sweet Chocolate Cake.

1 cup evaporated milk
1 cup sugar
3 egg yolks, slightly beaten
¼ lb. (½ cup) butter or margarine
1 tsp. vanilla
1⅓ cups (about) Baker's Angel Flake Coconut
1 cup chopped pecans

Combine milk, sugar, egg yolks, butter, and vanilla in a saucepan. Cook and stir over medium heat until thickened—about 12 minutes. Remove from heat. Add coconut and pecans. Beat until cool and thick enough to spread. Makes 2½ cups, or enough for tops of three 8- or 9-inch layers.

Fudge Cake

Perhaps this isn't the very first fudge cake recipe ever written but certainly it's one of the best, as two generations of good cooks will attest. Hershey Chocolate Company first printed it on their cocoa box label way back in the 1930's.

½ cup shortening
1½ cups sugar
2 eggs
1 tsp. vanilla
½ cup plus 1 Tbs. hot water
⅔ cup Hershey's Cocoa
1¾ cup unsifted all-purpose flour
1 tsp. baking soda
1 tsp. baking powder
½ tsp. salt
1 cup sour milk*

Grease bottoms and sides of two 9-inch layer pans. Cream shortening and sugar until fluffy. Add eggs, one at a time, beating well after each addition; blend in vanilla. Stir hot water into cocoa to form a smooth paste; gradually add to creamed mixture. Combine flour, baking soda, baking powder and salt; add alternately with sour milk to creamed mixture. Pour batter into pans. Bake at 350°F. for 30–35 minutes or until cake tester inserted in center comes out clean. Cool 10 minutes. Remove from pans; cool completely. Frost with your favorite frosting.

* *To Sour Milk:* Use 1 Tbs. vinegar plus milk to equal 1 cup.

Chocolate Town Special Cake

One of the best ever Chocolate Cake recipes to come from Chocolate Town, Hershey, Pennsylvania. A long-time favorite from the Hershey Cocoa box label.

½ cup Hershey's Cocoa
½ cup boiling water
⅔ cup shortening
1¾ cups sugar
1 tsp. vanilla

2 eggs
2¼ cups unsifted all-purpose flour
1½ tsps. baking soda
½ tsp. salt
1⅓ cups buttermilk or sour milk*

Grease and dust with flour two 9-inch cake pans. Make smooth paste of cocoa and boiling water; cool slightly. Cream shortening, sugar and vanilla in large mixer bowl; blend in eggs. Combine flour, baking soda and salt; add alternately with buttermilk to creamed mixture. Add cocoa paste to batter, blending well. Pour batter into pans. Bake at 350°F. for 35–40 minutes or until cake tester inserted in center comes out clean. Frost as desired.

*To Sour Milk: Use 1 Tbs. plus 1 tsp. vinegar plus milk to equal 1⅓ cups.

Golden Coconut Frosting

½ cup butter or margarine
1⅓ cups (about) Baker's Angel Flake Coconut**
1 cup firmly packed brown sugar
¼ cup milk
2 cups (about) sifted confectioners' sugar

Melt 2 Tbs. butter in a skillet. Add coconut and stir until golden brown. Remove about half the coconut; set aside. Melt remaining butter in skillet with coconut. Add brown sugar. Cook and stir over low heat 2 minutes, or until blended. Then add milk; bring to a boil. Remove from heat. Cool. Gradually add confectioners' sugar until it's the right consistency to spread, beating well after each addition. Spread on cake. Sprinkle with remaining

** Or use 1 cup Baker's Cookie Coconut

coconut. Makes 2 cups frosting, or enough to cover tops and sides of two 8-inch layers, one 9-inch square, or 24 cupcakes.

Glazed Chocolate Torte

Now there comes a time when only a real pretty "dress up" dinner party will suit the occasion and this is certainly the dessert to crown the meal. Beautiful—just beautiful. It's from the Hershey Baking Chocolate box.

¼ cup shortening
¾ cup sugar
3 egg yolks
1 tsp. vanilla
⅓ cup blanched ground almonds
3 blocks (3 ounces) Hershey's Baking Chocolate, melted

1 cup sifted all-purpose flour
½ tsp. baking powder
½ tsp. baking soda
½ tsp. salt
¾ cup milk, room temperature
3 egg whites
¼ cup sugar
Filling (below)
Glaze (below)

Cream shortening with sugar. Add egg yolks and vanilla; beat well. Stir in ground almonds, then baking chocolate. Sift together flour, baking powder, baking soda and salt. Add to creamed mixture alternately with milk, blending well after each addition. Beat egg whites until frothy, gradually add sugar and beat until stiff peaks form. Carefully fold into chocolate mixture and turn into two greased and cocoa-dusted 8-inch round layer pans. Bake at 350°F. for 20 minutes or until done. Cool 10 minutes; remove from pans. When completely cool, split layers and fill with whipped cream.

Filling: 1½ cups whipping cream, sweetened and whipped or 3 cups non-dairy whipped topping.

Glaze

1 block (1 oz.) Hershey's
  Baking Chocolate
2 Tbs. butter
1 Tbs. light corn syrup

1 cup confectioners' sugar
2 Tbs. hot water

Combine chocolate, butter and corn syrup in top of double boiler over simmering water. Stir in confectioners' sugar and hot water. While still warm, pour glaze over torte. Spread quickly, allowing glaze to run down the sides. Refrigerate until serving time.

Prize Coconut Cake

This is the recipe for coconut cake that so many people requested; "the one with coconut in the batter not just in the frosting." It first appeared in *Baker's Chocolate and Coconut Favorites* **cookbook in 1962. It's also in the latest edition and yes, it's just as good as you remembered.**

1¾ cups sifted cake flour
2¼ tsps. Calumet Baking Powder
 ¾ tsp. salt
 ½ cup butter or margarine
 1 cup plus 2 Tbs. sugar
 2 eggs
 ⅔ cup milk
 1 tsp. vanilla
 ⅔ cup Baker's Cookie or Angel Flake Coconut

Measure sifted flour, baking powder and salt; sift together. Cream butter. Gradually add sugar; cream until light and fluffy. Add eggs, one at a time, beating well after each addition. Alternately add flour mixture and milk, beating after each addition until smooth. Stir in vanilla and coconut. Pour batter into two 8-inch layer pans, lined on bottoms with paper. Bake in moderate oven (350°F.) 30–35 minutes. Cool in pans 10 minutes; then remove from pans and finish cooling on racks. Frost with Golden Coconut Frosting. (See recipe p. 159.)

Delicate Graham Cracker Cake

Do you remember this one? It's been one of Nabisco's most requested recipes for 40 years. Actually more of a torte than a cake. Fill and frost with sweetened whipped cream for a taste of old Vienna.

⅔ cup all-purpose flour
¾ cup granulated sugar
2½ tsps. baking powder
½ tsp. salt
1⅓ cups Nabisco Graham Cracker Crumbs
½ cup shortening
¾ cup milk
1 tsp. vanilla extract
2 eggs

Combine flour, sugar, baking powder, salt and Nabisco Graham Cracker Crumbs. Place shortening in a bowl. Add dry ingredients, milk and vanilla; mix until dry ingredients are moistened. Beat 2 minutes in electric mixer or 300 strokes by hand. Add eggs and beat 1 minute or 150 strokes by hand. Pour into 2 heavily greased 8-inch layer cake pans; bake in a preheated moderate oven (350°F.) about 25 minutes, or until done. Cool. Fill and frost as desired.

Peanut Butter Picnic Cake

An old favorite from Parkay Margarine. Children especially like it, I'm told, but so do the men in my life—every one of them from six to sixty years.

½ cup Parkay Margarine
1⅓ cups sugar
¼ cup peanut butter
2 eggs
1 tsp. vanilla
2 cups flour
1 Tbs. baking powder

1 tsp. salt
1 cup milk
1 10-oz. jar Kraft Strawberry
    Preserves or Grape Jelly
    Peanut Butter Frosting
    (below)

Cream margarine and sugar until light and fluffy. Blend in peanut butter, eggs and vanilla. Add combined dry ingredients alternately with milk, mixing well after each addition. Pour into two greased and floured 8- or 9-inch layer pans. Bake at 350°F., 35–40 minutes or until wooden pick inserted in center comes out clean. Cool 10 minutes; remove from pans. Spread ⅔ cup preserves between layers. Frost with Peanut Butter Frosting. Decorate with additional preserves.

Peanut Butter Frosting

¼ cup Parkay margarine
¼ cup peanut butter
1 tsp. vanilla
    Dash of salt

2½ cups sifted confectioners'
    sugar
3 Tbs. milk

Cream margarine; blend in peanut butter, vanilla and salt. Add sugar alternately with milk, beating until light and fluffy.

Tennessee Jam Cake

My Aunt Della made a version of this cake back in Memphis. It's a Southern tradition for Sunday dinner dessert. This one is from Kraft, who seem to have a "hand" with old-fashioned "receipts."

1 cup margarine
1½ cups granulated sugar
1 10-oz. jar Kraft
　Strawberry, Raspberry
　or Blackberry Preserves
4 eggs
2½ cups flour
　Brown Sugar Frosting
　(below)
　Confectioners' sugar

1 tsp. soda
1 tsp. nutmeg
1 tsp. cinnamon
1 tsp. cloves
¼ tsp. salt
1 cup buttermilk
1½ cups chopped pecans

Cream margarine and granulated sugar until light and fluffy. Blend in preserves and eggs. Add combined dry ingredients to creamed mixture, alternately with buttermilk, mixing well after each addition. Stir in nuts. Pour into three greased and floured 9-inch layer pans. Bake at 350°F., 30–35 minutes. Cool 10 minutes; remove from pans. Fill and frost sides with Brown Sugar Frosting. Sift confectioners' sugar over top of cake.

Brown Sugar Frosting: Combine 1 cup packed brown sugar, ½ cup margarine and ¼ cup milk; bring to boil, stirring constantly. Remove from heat; cool 10 minutes. Gradually add 3 cups sifted confectioners' sugar, beating until well blended.

Peach Upside-Down Cake

Upside-down cake was popular when Shirley Temple was a star, remember? I'm sure your mother does. This version, made with fresh peaches, is from the test kitchen of Parkay Margarine.

Parkay Margarine
½ cup packed brown sugar
1½ cups fresh peach slices
⅔ cup granulated sugar
1 egg

½ tsp. vanilla
1½ cups flour
1½ tsps. baking powder
½ tsp. salt
½ cup milk

Melt 3 Tbs. margarine in 8- or 9-inch oven-proof skillet or layer pan; sprinkle with brown sugar. Arrange fruit in skillet. Cream ⅓ cup margarine and granulated sugar until light and fluffy. Blend in egg and vanilla. Add combined dry ingredients alternately with milk, mixing well after each addition. Carefully pour batter over fruit. Bake at 350°F., 40– 45 minutes or until wooden pick inserted in center comes out clean. Immediately invert onto serving platter.

Variation: Substitute 16-oz. can peach slices, drained, for fresh peaches.

Fresh Apple Cake

A new cake from the Kellogg's kitchens destined to become an old favorite. The perfect afternoon snack cake. Great with icy cold milk, superb with freshly made steaming hot coffee.

1½ cups all-purpose flour
2 tsps. baking soda
½ tsp. salt

1 tsp. ground cinnamon
1 tsp. ground nutmeg

½ cup margarine or butter, softened
1 cup granulated sugar
2 eggs
4 cups finely chopped, pared apples
1 cup Kellogg's All-Bran® cereal or Kellogg's Bran Buds® cereal

1 3-oz. package cream cheese, softened
1 Tbs. margarine or butter, softened
1 tsp. vanilla flavoring
1½ cups sifted confectioners' sugar

Stir together flour, soda, salt, cinnamon and nutmeg. Beat the ½ cup margarine and the granulated sugar. Beat in eggs. Stir in apples, cereal and flour mixture. Spread in greased 9 × 9 × 2-inch baking pan. Bake at 350°F. about 45 minutes or until done.

To make frosting, beat cream cheese, the 1 Tbs. margarine and vanilla. Gradually add confectioners' sugar, beating until smooth. If frosting is too thick, add 1–2 tsps. milk. Spread on cooled cake. Yield 12 servings.

Variations: In place of Kellogg's All-Bran® cereal, use 2 cups Kellogg's 40% Bran Flakes® cereal. Or crush 1⅓ cups Kellogg's Cracklin' Bran® cereal to coarse crumbs.

Sun Maid® Raisin Nut Cake

A top request recipe since it first appeared on the Sun Maid® Raisin box over fifty years ago. Made to order for tea time and the coffee hour.

½ lb. self-raising flour
½ tsp. salt
1 tsp. mixed spices
2 oz. chopped nuts
4½ oz. Sun Maid® Seedless Raisins

4 oz. margarine
6 oz. granulated sugar
2 eggs

Grease and flour a loaf tin, 9½ × 5½ × 2½ inches. Sieve together first three ingredients and add the nuts and raisins. Cream the margarine and sugar thoroughly and add the eggs, one at a time, beating thoroughly after each addition. Add the flour mixture alternately with the milk, beating well after each addition, and bake in the prepared tin in a moderate oven (350°F.) for about 1–1¼ hours.

Orange-Raisin Whole Wheat Cake

Several years ago a Pillsbury Bake-Off® winner and a real star. People love it, it's one of the new "mix-it-all-in-one-bowl" cakes, made with whole wheat flour and just delicious.

1¼ cups Pillsbury's Best® All-Purpose Flour
 1 cup Pillsbury's Best® Whole Wheat Flour
 1 cup brown sugar
 1 tsp. baking soda
 ½ tsp. salt
 1 cup orange juice
 ½ cup oil
 1 tsp. grated orange rind
 1 egg
 ½ cup raisins

Heat oven to 350°F. Grease and flour 8- or 9-inch square pan. Combine all ingredients except raisins; beat 2 minutes at medium speed. Stir in raisins. Pour into prepared pan. Bake at 350°F. for 40–50 minutes or until toothpick inserted in center comes out clean. Serve with Honey-Nut Topping, if desired. Makes 9 servings.

Honey-Nut Topping

1 Tbs. cornstarch
½ cup chopped walnuts
½ cup water

½ cup honey
½ cup butter

In small saucepan, combine cornstarch and honey; add remaining ingredients. Cook over medium heat, stirring constantly, until mixture starts to boil. Continue cooking and stirring about 1 minute or until slightly thickened. Serve warm. Makes 1¾ cups.

Fruit Gâteau

Pretty and so simple. A light-as-air sponge cake layer topped with fresh seasonal fruit, an especially pretty idea for a summer party dessert. (I like fresh peaches best.) An old favorite from the Argo Cornstarch box.

2 eggs
⅓ cup sugar
¼ tsp. salt
⅓ cup sifted flour
¼ cup Argo or Kingsford's Corn Starch
2 cups assorted fresh fruit (mandarin oranges, sliced strawberries, peaches, apricot halves, grapes, etc.)
Glaze (below)
Whipped cream

Grease 9 × 1½-inch round layer pan. Line with waxed paper and grease again. In small bowl with mixer at high speed beat eggs until fluffy. Gradually add sugar and salt; beat until mixture is doubled in bulk and mounds slightly when dropped from a spoon, about 5 minutes. Sift flour and corn starch over egg mixture; thoroughly fold in. Pour into prepared pan. Bake in

350°F. oven 25 minutes or until cake springs back when lightly touched. Cool 10 minutes. Remove from pan; cool completely on wire rack. Place on serving plate. Arrange fruit as desired on top of sponge layer. Spoon glaze evenly over fruit. Let set 30 minutes. Garnish with whipped cream. Makes 8 servings.

Glaze: In small saucepan mix together 1 Tbs. corn starch, 1 cup apple juice and 1 Tbs. lemon juice. Stirring constantly, bring to boil over medium heat and boil 1 minute. Cool. Makes 1 cup.

Boston Cream Pie

This is a marvelous cake, one of America's best! Yes, this recipe did indeed originate in, or around, Boston and it's called a pie because "my dear, Boston pies are so elegant they are made with delicate cake layers instead of just plain pie crusts," or so I was told by a Boston lady. Hershey cooks perfected this version.

2 cups unsifted all-purpose flour	¼ cup shortening
1½ cups sugar	1½ tsps. vanilla
1 tsp. baking soda	1¼ cups buttermilk or sour milk*
1 tsp. baking powder	4 egg whites (reserve 2 egg yolks for filling)
½ tsp. salt	Cream Filling (below)
¼ cup butter or margarine, softened	Chocolate Glaze (below)

Grease and dust with flour two 9-inch layer pans. Combine flour, sugar, baking soda, baking powder and salt in large mixer bowl. Add butter, shortening, vanilla and buttermilk. Blend on low speed 30 seconds; beat on me-

* *To Sour Milk:* Use 1 Tbs. plus 1 tsp. vinegar plus milk to equal 1¼ cups.

dium speed 2 minutes. Add egg whites; beat 2 minutes. Pour into pans and bake at 350°F. for 30–35 minutes or until cake tester inserted in center comes out clean. Cool 10 minutes; remove from pans. Cool completely.

Prepare Cream Filling. Spoon onto 1 cake layer. Carefully top with remaining layer. Prepare Chocolate Glaze. Immediately pour onto top of cake, allowing some to drizzle down side. Chill before serving. Makes 8–10 servings.

Cream Filling: Combine ⅓ cup sugar, 2 Tbs. cornstarch and ⅛ tsp. salt in saucepan. Gradually add 1½ cups milk and reserved 2 egg yolks; blend well. Cook and stir over medium heat until mixture boils; boil and stir 1 minute. Remove from heat; blend in 1 Tbs. butter and 1 tsp. vanilla. Cool 10 minutes.

Chocolate Glaze: Combine 3 Tbs. water and 2 Tbs. butter in small saucepan. Bring to full boil; remove from heat and add ¼ cup Hershey's Cocoa. Stir until mixture leaves side of pan and forms ball. Beat in 1 cup confectioners' sugar and ½ tsp. vanilla until smooth.

Apple Pie with Cheese Topper

It's hard to imagine anything better to eat than a first-rate apple pie. And if ever one tasted a first-rate apple pie this is it; sweet but not too sweet, juicy but not too juicy, with a crust that is flaky and delicately brown. It's a perfect pie made even more perfect with a creamy Cheese Topping. The Crisco people tell me this recipe has received fan letters for years.

Crisco pastry for double-crust 9-inch pie
½ cup light raisins (optional)
6–8 tart apples, peeled, cored and sliced (6 cups)
½ tsp. grated lemon peel
1 tsp. lemon juice
¾ cup sugar
2 Tbs. flour
½ tsp. ground nutmeg
Dash salt
Cheese Topper (below)

Preheat oven to 400°F. Line a 9-inch pie plate with pastry. Pour boiling water over raisins and let stand 5 minutes; drain. Toss apples with lemon peel, juice and drained raisins. Combine sugar, flour, nutmeg and salt; mix with apples. Turn into pastry-lined pie plate. Place top crust over apples; seal and flute edges. Cut slits for escape of steam. Bake at 400°F. for 50–60 minutes or till done. Cover edges with foil after 15 minutes to prevent over-browning. Serve warm pie with Cheese Topper.

Cheese Topper: Have ½ cup (2 oz.) shredded Cheddar cheese and 1 package (3 oz.) cream cheese at room temperature. In small mixing bowl, combine cheeses and 2 Tbs. milk; beat till fluffy and nearly smooth.

Crunchy Pecan Pie

I'm not really sure about this recipe—is it a torte or is it a pie? One thing I am sure about, it's absolutely delicious and it's a snap to make. From the Nabisco Graham Cracker box, first printed in the 1940's.

3 egg whites
1 cup granulated sugar
12 squares Nabisco Graham Crackers, finely
    rolled (about 1 cup crumbs)
1 cup finely chopped pecans
¼ tsp. baking powder
1 cup heavy cream, whipped

Beat egg whites until soft peaks form; gradually add
sugar, beating until stiff peaks form. Combine next three
ingredients; fold into egg whites. Spread in a greased
9-inch pie plate. Bake in the center of preheated oven
(350°F.) 30 minutes. Cool thoroughly. Spread with whipped cream. Chill 6 hours or overnight. Makes 8 3¾-inch
wedges.

Southern Coconut Pie

**A rich custard pie, lavish with coconut. The recipe was per-
fected by home economists at the Baker Coconut test kitchens. Southerners tell me it's the real thing.**

2 Tbs. melted butter
⅓ cup sugar
¼ tsp. salt
3 eggs, slightly beaten
1 cup light corn syrup
1 tsp. vanilla
½ tsp. almond extract
⅔ cup Baker's Cookie Coconut
1 unbaked 9-inch pie shell

Blend butter, sugar and salt. Add eggs, syrup and extracts; stir well. Sprinkle coconut over bottom of pie shell. Pour filling over coconut. Bake in moderate oven (375°F.) 40–50 minutes. Cool. Serve with ice cream, prepared Dream Whip Whipped Topping or whipped cream, if desired. Makes 6–8 servings.

Chocolate Meringue Pie

Here, by insistent requests, is that "noble chocolate pie with the high and haughty meringue"—the chocolate pie that man in your life remembers. The recipe was first printed in *Baker's Chocolate and Coconut Favorites* **cookbook in 1962. Today even after 18 years it's still a top favorite.**

1¼ cups sugar
  3 Tbs. cornstarch
  ½ tsp. salt
  2 cups milk
1½ squares Baker's Unsweetened Chocolate,
    chopped
  2 egg yolks, slightly beaten
  1 Tbs. butter
  1 tsp. vanilla
  1 baked 8-inch pie shell, cooled
  2 egg whites

Mix 1 cup sugar, the cornstarch and salt in a saucepan. Gradually stir in milk. Add chocolate; cook and stir over medium heat until mixture comes to a boil and is thickened. Then continue to cook and stir 1 minute longer. Remove from heat. Gradually stir at least half of the hot mixture into egg yolks. Then stir egg yolk mixture into mixture in saucepan. Cook and stir 1 minute longer. Remove from heat. Blend in butter and vanilla. Cool 20 minutes; then beat just until smooth—about 30 seconds.

Pour into pie shell. Beat egg whites until foamy. Add ¼ cup sugar, a little at a time, beating well after each addition. Continue beating until stiff peaks will form. Spread over filling, carefully sealing to crust. Bake in hot oven (425°F.) 6–8 minutes, or until browned. Cool about 4 hours. Makes 6 servings.

Raisin Nut Pie

Raisin Nut Pie was among the winners in a Karo Corn Syrup contest held several years ago. You'll know why when you try it. Eunice Yeager of Lanesville, Indiana, sent in the recipe.

3 eggs
¾ cup Karo Dark Corn Syrup
½ cup firmly packed light brown sugar
¼ cup Mazola Margarine, melted
1 tsp. vanilla
¼ tsp. salt
1 cup raisins
½ cup chopped pecans or walnuts
1 unbaked (9-inch) pastry shell

In bowl beat eggs slightly. Stir in corn syrup, brown sugar, margarine, vanilla and salt. Stir in raisins and nuts. Turn into pastry shell. Bake in 350°F. oven 40–50 minutes or until knife inserted half-way between center and edge comes out clean. Cool on wire rack. If desired, serve with unsweetened whipped cream or vanilla ice cream. Makes 8 servings.

Vanilla Cream Pie

How long has it been since you've made a creamy, smooth egg custard pie? This is the original recipe and it's just as good now as it was in the 1940's when Argo and Kingsford first printed it on their cornstarch box.

⅔ cup sugar
¼ cup Argo or Kingsford's Corn Starch
½ tsp. salt
2½ cups milk
3 eggs, separated
1 tsp. vanilla
1 baked (9-inch) pastry shell
6 Tbs. sugar

In 2-quart saucepan mix together ⅔ cup sugar, cornstarch and salt. Gradually stir in milk until smooth. Stir in egg yolks, slightly beaten. Stirring constantly, bring to boil over medium-low heat and boil 1 minute. Remove from heat. Stir in vanilla. Cover surface with waxed paper or plastic wrap. Cool slightly (no longer than 1 hour). Turn filling into pastry shell. In small bowl with mixer at high speed beat egg whites until frothy peaks form. Gradually beat in 6 Tbs. sugar until stiff peaks form. Spread over filling sealing to edge of crust. Bake in 350°F. oven 15 to 20 minutes or until lightly browned. Cool at room temperature away from drafts. Makes 8 servings.

Banana Cream Pie: Follow recipe for Vanilla Cream Pie. Fill pastry shell with small amount of cooled filling. Arrange 2 bananas, sliced, over filling and cover with remaining filling.

Coconut Cream Pie: Follow recipe for Vanilla Cream Pie. Fold ¾ cup flaked coconut into cooled filling and sprinkle meringue with ¼ cup flaked coconut before baking. Bake in 425°F. oven 5 minutes or until meringue browns and coconut is toasted.

Chocolate Cream Pie: Follow recipe for Vanilla Cream Pie adding 2 squares (1 oz. each) unsweetened chocolate to milk mixture before cooking.

Impossible Coconut Pie

Here's a fantastic recipe from the Bisquick® Baking Mix box. It's so easy and so much fun to make. Try it once and it will become a favorite at your house.

    2 cups milk
    ¾ cup sugar
    ½ cup Bisquick® Baking Mix
    ¼ cup margarine or butter
    4 eggs
 1½ tsps. vanilla
    1 cup flaked or shredded coconut

Heat oven to 350°F. Lightly grease pie plate, 9 × 1¼ inches. Place all ingredients in blender container. Cover and blend on high speed 15 seconds. Pour into pie plate. Bake until golden brown and knife inserted in center comes out clean, 50–55 minutes. Refrigerate any remaining pie.

Impossible Chocolate Pie: Add 2 Tbs. cocoa.

Impossible Fruit Pie: Use 10-inch pie plate. Cool pie; spread 1 21-oz. can fruit pie filling over top. Refrigerate at least 2 hours.

Impossible Lemon Pie: Use 10-inch pie plate. Add ¼ cup lemon juice.

Impossible Macaroon Pie: Do not blend coconut; sprinkle over top of pie before baking.

Mystery Torte

"My mother used to make a pie with Saltine Crackers called a Mystery Torte. Do you have a recipe?" The Nabisco Company has been getting letters like this for years. They always write back, "Yes, we do!" And here it is:

10 Premium Saltine Crackers, coarsely rolled
   (about ⅔ cup crumbs)
½ cup chopped pecans
   Chocolate-Cream Topping (optional—below)
½ tsp. baking powder
3 egg whites (at room temperature)
1 cup granulated sugar
½ tsp. vanilla extract

Combine cracker crumbs and pecans. Set aside. Add baking powder to egg whites. Beat until soft peaks form. Gradually add sugar and vanilla. Continue beating until egg whites are very stiff and glossy, but not dry. Fold in cracker mixture. Turn into 1 9-inch ungreased pie plate. Bake in a preheated oven (300°F.) 50 minutes. Chill several hours.

Chocolate-Cream Topping: For an excellent topping, combine ½ cup heavy cream with 3 Tbs. confectioners' sugar and 3 tsps. instant cocoa mix. Whip until stiff. Spoon over just before serving. Makes 4–6 servings.

Pumpkin Chiffon Pie

Here is the recipe for that "lighter" pumpkin pie that so many people told me is better than best. The secret of its lightness is the Knox Unflavored Gelatine. It is indeed such a lovely holiday pie.

1 envelope Knox
   Unflavored Gelatine
¾ cup brown sugar
½ tsp. salt
½ tsp. nutmeg
1 tsp. cinnamon
3 eggs, separated

¾ cup milk
1 16-oz. can pumpkin
¼ cup sugar
9-inch baked pastry shell

In medium saucepan, mix Unflavored Gelatine, brown sugar, salt and spices; blend in egg yolks beaten with milk. Let stand 1 minute. Stir over low heat until Gelatine is completely dissolved, about 8 minutes; blend in pumpkin. Pour into large bowl and chill, stirring occasionally, until mixture mounds slightly when dropped from spoon. In medium bowl, beat egg whites until soft peaks form; gradually add sugar and beat until stiff. Fold into Gelatine mixture. Turn into prepared crust and chill until firm. Garnish, if desired, with whipped cream. Makes about 8 servings.

Brandy Alexander Pie

Brandy Alexanders were a favorite drink concocted in the 1920's during prohibition. The pie came later—about 1950—thanks to the Knox Gelatine good cooks and it proved to be almost as much of a sensation.

2 envelopes Knox Unflavored Gelatine
¾ cup cold whipping or heavy cream
¾ cup milk, heated to boiling
¼ cup sugar
3 Tbs. brandy
3 Tbs. creme de cacao
1 cup ice cubes (about 6–8)
Chocolate-Coconut Crust (below) or 9-inch graham cracker crust

In 5-cup blender, sprinkle Unflavored Gelatine over chilled cream; let stand 3–4 minutes. Add hot milk and process at low speed until gelatine is completely dissolved, about 2 minutes. Add sugar, brandy and creme de cacao; process at high speed until blended. Add ice cubes, one at a time; process at high speed until ice is melted. Pour into prepared crust and chill until firm. Garnish, if desired, with maraschino cherries. Makes about 8 servings.

Chocolate-Coconut Crust: In medium bowl, combine one square (1 oz.) unsweetened chocolate, melted, and 2 Tbs. milk; stir in 2 cups flaked coconut and ½ cup confectioners' sugar. Press into 9-inch pie pan.

Mr. & Mrs. Foster's Yogurt Pie

Pearl Byrd Foster developed this recipe for her famous American style New York restaurant. Although it's new on the scene, Dannon Yogurt has brought this pie hundreds of fans. It's sure to go down in history as an all-time favorite dessert.

1 Tbs. unflavored gelatin*
¼ cup cold water
2 egg yolks, slightly beaten
¼ cup milk
2 cups Dannon Plain Yogurt
1 tsp. Vanilla
8 oz. Neufchatel** cheese, room temperature

8 oz. cream cheese, room temperature
1 tsp. molasses
1 Tbs. clover honey
½ cup graham cracker crumbs
1 graham cracker crumb shell

Soften gelatin in cold water and dissolve over hot water. Add milk to the slightly beaten egg yolks and cook with the gelatin over gently boiling water until it coats a silver spoon. Set aside to cool. Cream the cheese, vanilla, molasses and honey together (if mixing machine used—cream on low speed only), add one cup of Dannon Yogurt and continue to cream until smooth. Pour the cold gelatin mixture slowly over the cheese, stirring constantly. Add the second cup of Dannon Yogurt. Mix well. Pour into baked graham cracker crumb shell and chill until firm. When ready to serve, sprinkle top with graham cracker crumbs. Makes 1 10-inch pie.

* If a softer filling is desired—use less gelatin.
** If Neufchatel is not available, you may substitute an additional 8 oz. cream cheese.

Alaska Pie

Baked Alaska was a featured dessert at Delmonicos Restaurant in old New York. Kraft perfected this easy adaptation.

1½ cups graham cracker
  crumbs
 3 Tbs. sugar
 6 Tbs. margarine, melted
 1 qt. ice cream, softened*

3 egg whites
  Dash of salt
1 cup Kraft Marshmallow
  Creme

Combine crumbs, sugar and margarine; press onto bottom and sides of 9-inch pie plate. Bake at 375°F., 8 minutes. Cool. Fill crust with softened ice cream. Freeze. Beat egg whites and salt until soft peaks form. Gradually add marshmallow creme, beating until stiff peaks form. Spread over frozen ice cream pie, sealing to edge of crust. Bake at 500°F., 3 minutes or until lightly browned. Serve immediately.

To Make Ahead: Prepare recipe as directed, except for final baking. Freeze several hours or overnight. When ready to serve, bake as directed.

* Almost any ice cream is delicious in this meringue-topped pie. Try fresh peach, strawberry, chocolate, fudge-nut or New York cherry.

Easy Fruit Tarts

You know those beautiful little glistening fruit tarts that look so beguiling but sound so difficult to make? Well, Jell-O has made them easy. If you would like to make your reputation as a great hostess, serve these at your next party.

 1 3¼-oz. package Jell-O Vanilla Pudding and
   Pie Filling
 8 baked 3-inch tart shells (frozen, packaged, or
   home-baked)
1–2 cups assorted fruit (see suggested fruits
   below)
 1 3-oz. package Jell-O Strawberry, Raspberry
   or Orange Gelatin

Prepare pudding as directed on package; chill. Divide evenly among tart shells. Top with any of the fruit combinations below, arranging in neat design. Chill. Meanwhile, prepare gelatin as directed on package. Chill until thickened. Spoon gelatin over tarts, using just enough to cover fruit with a smooth glaze. Chill until ready to serve. Pour remaining gelatin into serving dish and chill to use at another time. Garnish with prepared Dream Whip Whipped Topping or whipped cream, if desired. Makes 8 tarts.

Note: Recipe may be doubled for party serving.

Suggested fruits:

Blueberries and grapes
Blueberries and peaches
Strawberries and green grapes
Strawberries and bananas
Blueberries and green grapes
Green grapes and mandarin orange sections
Canned pineapple slice with stemmed Bing Cherry in center

Blueberries with whole strawberry in center
Apricot halves garnished with mint sprigs
Layered peach slices
Whole strawberries

9.
Dessert
Sampler

Americans have a national sweet tooth. Not for us the chaste piece of fruit or the oh-so-elegant wedge of cheese. Both may be simply splendid in their place, but for ending a meal, I join my fellow Americans in preferring a nice, gooey sweet finale. So here are some of the gooey-est and the best.

We lead off with three elegant soufflés; the first, a hot soufflé—chocolate, of course. The time was when hot soufflés were a "chancy" thing, but not this one. Like all our carefully tested food company recipes, the "chance" has been thoroughly tested out. Then there are a pair of easy cold soufflés, elegant enough to serve a queen, followed by a coconut sponge roll and a divine shortcake to swath in clouds of marshmallow and whipped cream; and, because I know we all love chocolate, there are four super chocolate specials. I haven't neglected the simple desserts either. There are old-fashioned Brown Betty and lemon pudding, plus a group of ever-popular gelatin recipes, followed by America's all-time favorite dessert—ice cream with a bunch of really great recipes that are easy, inexpensive, and sinfully good.

Memories are made of desserts: Mom's apple pie is remembered long after the chicken and dumplings are forgotten, and who can forget the homemade ice cream that followed every summer Sunday dinner? Back in Louisiana, we made it in an old-fashioned hand churn. As soon as everyone returned from church, the custard was poured into the ice cream can, the churn packed with ice and salt, and the churning began. Once stiff enough, the dasher was removed (I always tried to get a taste) and the ice cream was allowed to mellow while we consumed our Sunday chicken and iced tea. Then the ice cream appeared—generous big bowls of it—cold and sweet with a heavenly creaminess, loaded with fresh peaches or figs. It was a dessert to dream about.

Happily, now you can whip up memorable desserts in no time. New easy recipes, new methods and new equipment make it simple to crown every meal with a great dessert. To make life even sweeter our food companies have given us a Dessert Sampler representing their very best handiwork like the stitched samplers of long ago. All you have to do is enjoy!

SOUFFLÉS

Some like it hot—some like it cold—but everyone loves a dessert soufflé and believe it or not the experts at Kraft have made dessert soufflés fail proof. Honest, you can't miss. Cooks everywhere have been whipping them up successfully for at least ten years.

Chocolate "Philly" Soufflé

2 Tbs. margarine
2 Tbs. flour
½ cup milk
½ tsp. salt
1 8-oz. package
  Philadelphia Brand
  Cream Cheese, cubed

⅔ cup sugar
2 1-oz. squares
  unsweetened chocolate,
  melted
1½ tsps. vanilla
4 eggs, separated

Make a white sauce with margarine, flour, milk and salt. Add cream cheese, ⅓ cup sugar, chocolate and vanilla; stir over low heat until smooth. Remove from heat. Gradually add slightly beaten egg yolks; cool slightly. Beat egg whites until soft peaks form. Gradually add remaining sugar, beating until stiff peaks form. Fold cream cheese mixture into egg whites. Pour into 1¼-quart soufflé dish or casserole. Bake at 350°F. for 1 hour. Serve immediately. Makes 6 servings.

Strawberry Romanoff Soufflé

1 envelope unflavored
  gelatin
¼ cup cold water

1 8-oz. package cream
  cheese
1 10-oz. package frozen
  strawberries, thawed

¼ cup Cointreau liqueur
2 egg whites
1 7-oz. jar Kraft
Marshmallow Creme

1 cup heavy cream,
whipped

Combine gelatin and water in saucepan; let stand 1 minute. Stir over medium heat until dissolved. Gradually add to softened cream cheese, mixing until well blended. Stir in strawberries and liqueur; chill until slightly thickened. Beat egg whites until soft peaks form. Gradually add marshmallow creme, beating until stiff peaks form. Fold in egg white mixture and whipped cream into gelatin mixture. Wrap a 3-inch collar of aluminum foil around top of 1-quart soufflé dish; secure with tape. Pour mixture into dish; chill until firm. Remove foil collar before serving. Makes 8–10 servings.

Variation: Frozen raspberries can be substituted for strawberries.

Caramel Praline Soufflé

1 envelope unflavored
gelatin
1½ cups cold water
28 Kraft Caramels
2 Tbs. sugar
5 eggs, separated

1 cup heavy cream,
whipped
2 Tbs. sugar
¼ cup chopped pecans,
toasted

Combine gelatin and ½ cup cold water. Melt caramels and sugar with remaining water in saucepan over low heat. Stir frequently until sauce is smooth. Stir small amount of hot mixture into egg yolks; return to hot mixture. Cook 3–5 minutes over low heat, stirring constantly, until thickened. Stir in gelatin. Cool to room temperature.

Fold stiffly beaten egg whites and whipped cream into caramel mixture. Wrap a 3-inch collar of aluminum foil around top of 1-quart soufflé dish; secure with tape. Pour mixture into dish; chill until firm. Remove foil collar before serving.

Melt sugar in skillet over medium heat until clear and caramel colored. Stir in nuts; spoon onto greased cookie sheet. Immediately separate nuts with two forks. Cool; break into small pieces. Sprinkle over soufflé before serving. Makes 6 servings.

Coconut Sponge Roll

A simply beautiful and very festive dessert. Sensational for a party. Baker's Coconut test kitchens made it easy!

¾ tsp. Calumet Baking Powder
½ tsp. salt
 4 eggs (at room temperature)
¾ cup sugar
¾ cup sifted cake flour
 1 tsp. vanilla
   Coconut Whipped Cream (below)
½ cup Baker's Coconut

Combine baking powder, salt and eggs in bowl. Beat, gradually adding sugar, until mixture becomes thick and light colored. Gradually fold in sifted flour; add vanilla. Line a 15 × 10 × 1-inch jelly roll pan on bottom with paper; then grease sides and paper. Pour batter into pan. Bake in a hot oven (400°F.) for 13 minutes.

Turn cake out onto cloth, which has been sprinkled with confectioners' sugar. Quickly remove paper and cut off crisp edges of cake. Then roll cake, rolling cloth up in cake. Let stand on cake rack about 30 minutes. Unroll cake, spread about 2 cups of Coconut Whipped Cream on roll and roll again. Spread with remaining filling and sprinkle with coconut. Chill.

Coconut Whipped Cream

1½ cups whipping cream   ¾ tsp. vanilla
1 Tbs. confectioners' sugar   ½ cup Baker's Coconut

Combine all ingredients in a chilled bowl. Whip cream until thick but still glossy. (Do not overbeat.) Makes about 3 cups, or enough to top a 13 × 9 × 2-inch cake, two 9-inch layers, or to fill and frost a cake roll.

Shortcake Supreme

I've always said that no one could improve an old-fashioned shortcake; well, now I take it all back. This super shortcake is just fabulous. Kraft featured it on their television series and it has gotten raves ever since.

2 cups flour
2 Tbs. sugar
1 Tbs. baking powder
½ tsp. salt
1 egg, slightly beaten
⅔ cup milk
½ cup Parkay Margarine,
    melted

1 cup Kraft Marshmallow
    Creme
1 cup heavy cream,
    whipped
1 tsp. vanilla
1½ cups peach slices
1½ cups strawberry slices
½ cup blueberries

Combine dry ingredients. Add combined egg, milk and margarine, mixing just until moistened. Spread into greased and floured 8-inch layer pan. Bake at 450°F., 12–15 minutes or until golden brown. Cool 10 minutes; remove from pan. Cool.

Combine marshmallow creme, 2 Tbs. heavy cream and vanilla; mix until well blended. Whip remaining heavy cream until stiff. Fold in marshmallow creme mixture. Split shortcake in half horizontally; fill with half of fruit and marshmallow creme mixture. Top with remaining fruit and marshmallow creme mixture. Makes 8–10 servings.

Fudgy Casserole à la Mode

Do you have children? Or a husband? Make them all happy with this chocolatey chocolate dessert. It's been an easy-to-make favorite since Hershey printed it on their Baking Chocolate box a dozen years ago.

  3 blocks (3 oz.) Hershey's Baking Chocolate
 ½ cup + 1 Tbs. butter or margarine, softened
1½ cups sugar
  3 eggs
1½ tsps. vanilla
 ¾ cup sifted all-purpose flour
 ¾ cup chopped pecans
    Vanilla ice cream

Melt baking chocolate in top of a double boiler over simmering water. Remove from heat. Beat in butter or margarine, sugar, eggs and vanilla. Blend in flour; add chopped pecans. Pour into buttered 1- or 1½-quart casserole. Bake at 350°F. for 55 minutes. Spoon into individual dishes and serve warm with ice cream. Makes 6–8 servings.

Brandied Cherry Chocolate Mousse

One of the most popular recipes to ever appear on the Hershey Chocolate package in the last 20 years.

1 cup pitted, dark sweet cherries, drained
  (reserve juice)
¼ cup brandy or cherry juice
3 blocks (3 oz.) Hershey's Baking Chocolate
⅓ cup cherry juice
1 cup sugar
3 egg yolks, well beaten
2 cups whipping cream, sweetened and
  whipped

Cut cherries into quarters. Pour brandy over cherries and marinate several hours. (If using cherry juice, no need to marinate.) Melt baking chocolate with ⅓ cup cherry juice in saucepan, stirring constantly over medium-low heat. Add sugar; cook until dissolved. Gradually stir hot mixture into egg yolks. Return to saucepan and cook until mixture boils. Cool. Drain cherries and stir brandy or ¼ cup juice into chocolate mixture. Carefully fold chocolate mixture into whipped cream. Fold in cherries and pour into oiled 1½-quart bowl. Cover; freeze overnight. At serving time, remove from freezer; let stand 10 minutes. Loosen with spatula and unmold. Cut 10–12 wedges and serve.

Chocolate Pudding

This is what I call a "comforting recipe"—real, honest, made with milk and eggs, chocolate pudding to enjoy and remember because it's been around since the 1920's when Hershey printed it on their Baking Chocolate box.

1 cup sugar
¼ cup cornstarch
½ tsp. salt
2½ cups milk
3 egg yolks, well-beaten
2 blocks (2 oz.) Hershey's Baking Chocolate
1 Tbs. butter
1 tsp. vanilla

Combine sugar, cornstarch and salt in medium saucepan; gradually stir in milk and egg yolks. Add baking chocolate, broken into pieces; cook and stir over medium heat until mixture boils. Boil and stir one minute; remove from heat. Add butter and vanilla; pour into individual serving dishes. Chill. Serve with sweetened whipped cream topping. Makes 6 servings.

Mt. Gretna Chocolate Fondue

When this recipe appeared on the Hershey Chocolate package its reputation spread fast—here was a Chocolate Fondue that was rich as sin but didn't become too thick while waiting to be dipped into.

3½ blocks (3½ oz.) Hershey's Baking Chocolate
1¼ cups (14-oz. can) sweetened condensed milk
½ cup marshmallow creme
1 Tbs. milk
1½ tsps. vanilla
1 Tbs. creamy peanut butter (optional)

Combine baking chocolate and condensed milk in saucepan; stir constantly over medium-low heat until chocolate is melted and mixture is smooth. Blend in marshmallow creme and milk. Just before serving, stir in vanilla and peanut butter. Transfer to fondue pot. Makes 2 cups.

Serve by dipping any of the following into warm fondue: Apple, pear, peach or banana slices; strawberries, pineapple chunks, mandarin orange segments, cherries, nut halves, marshmallows, ladyfingers, pieces of angel food or pound cake.

Sun-Maid® Raisin Brown Betty

Developed in the 1930's before World War II, this old-fashioned favorite appeared on the Sun-Maid® box almost 50 years ago.

 3 cups finely chopped tart apples
 1 cup Sun-Maid® Seedless Raisins
 ½ cup brown sugar (packed)
 ¼ tsp. nutmeg
 ¼ tsp. cinnamon
 1 cup soft bread crumbs
 1 Tbs. butter
 ⅓ cup water

Arrange alternating layers of apples and raisins in greased baking dish. Sprinkle each layer with sugar blended with nutmeg and cinnamon. Add water. Top with crumbs mixed with melted butter. Cover. Bake in hot oven (400°F.) 30–40 minutes until apples are tender. Remove cover and continue baking to brown top. Serve with cream or hard sauce. Makes 6 servings.

Saucy Lemon Pudding

An old-fashioned favorite, this pudding separates as it bakes into a delicate sponge layer and a creamy lemon sauce. A Parkay "1965 classic."

⅓ cup Parkay Margarine
1 cup sugar
2 eggs, separated
2 Tbs. lemon juice
1 Tbs. grated lemon rind
⅓ cup flour
1 cup milk

Cream margarine and ¾ cup sugar until light and fluffy. Blend in egg yolks, lemon juice and rind. Add flour; mix well. Stir in milk. Beat egg whites until soft peaks form. Gradually add remaining sugar, beating until stiff peaks form. Fold into batter; pour into 8 6-oz. custard cups. Set custard cups in baking pan; pour in boiling water to ½-inch depth. Bake at 350°F., 35–40 minutes. Remove from water; cool 10 minutes. Invert on dessert dishes. Makes 8 servings.

Variation: Prepare recipe as directed. Pour batter into 1-quart casserole. Bake at 350°F., 40–45 minutes. Cool 20 minutes; invert on serving plate.

Banana Pudding

Remember home-made Banana Pudding? Most Southerners do. This is the real thing, made from scratch. The recipe, a consistent favorite, was on the Nabisco Nilla Wafers package way back when I was a child.

¾ cup sugar, granulated
3 Tbs. all-purpose flour
Dash of salt
4 eggs
2 cups milk
½ tsp. vanilla extract
Nabisco Nilla Wafers
5–6 medium size fully ripe bananas, sliced

Combine ½ cup sugar, flour and salt in top of double boiler. Mix in 1 whole egg and 3 egg yolks. Stir in milk. Cook, uncovered, over boiling water, stirring constantly, until thickened. Remove from heat; add vanilla. Spread small amount on bottom of 1½-quart casserole; cover with layer of Nilla Wafers. Top with layer of sliced bananas. Pour about ⅓ of custard over bananas. Continue to layer wafers, bananas and custard to make 3 layers of each ending with custard. Beat remaining 3 egg whites until stiff, but not dry; gradually add remaining ¼ cup sugar and beat until mixture forms stiff peaks. Pile on top of pudding covering entire surface. Bake in preheated hot oven (425°F.) 5 minutes or until delicately browned. Serve warm or chilled. Makes 8 (about ¾-cup) servings.

Basic Vanilla Chiffon

The Knox Company has been inserting this extra-easy recipe in their Gelatine package for dozens of years. It's such a favorite with "creative" cooks who want to do their "own thing" with special flavoring and such that it simply can't be left out.

1 envelope Knox Unflavored Gelatine
¼ cup sugar
2 eggs, separated
1¾ cups milk
1 tsp. vanilla extract

In medium saucepan, mix Unflavored Gelatine with 2 Tbs. sugar; blend in egg yolks beaten with milk. Let stand 1 minute. Stir over low heat until Gelatine is completely dissolved, about 5 minutes; add vanilla. Pour into large bowl and chill, stirring occasionally, until mixture mounds slightly when dropped from spoon. In medium bowl, beat egg whites until soft peaks form; gradually add remaining sugar and beat until stiff. Fold into Gelatine mixture. Turn into 4-cup bowl or dessert dishes and chill until set. Makes about 8 servings.

Variations:

Chocolate Chiffon: After Gelatine is completely dissolved, stir in ½ cup semi-sweet chocolate chips. Continue cooking, stirring constantly, until chocolate is melted. With wire whip or rotary beater, beat mixture until chocolate is blended.

Coffee Chiffon: Mix 1 Tbs. instant coffee powder with Gelatine and sugar.

Lemon Chiffon: Omit vanilla. After Gelatine is completely dissolved, cool mixture completely. Add 2 Tbs. lemon juice and 2 tsps. grated lemon peel.

Peppermint Chiffon: Substitute ¼ tsp. peppermint extract for vanilla; if desired, add a few drops red food coloring.

Soufflé: Turn the chiffon mixture into a soufflé dish, using a collar for the characteristic high-rise effect. To make collar, fold foil into four thicknesses 3 inches wide and long enough to go around the soufflé dish with generous overlap. Attach to dish with tape, leaving collar 2 inches higher than rim of dish. The volume of the Gelatine mixture should be about 4 cups more than the volume of the dish without the collar.

Charlotte: Turn chiffon mixture into a bowl, loaf pan or spring-form pan lined with lady fingers. For an 8-inch bowl you need about 12 ladyfingers. Split ladyfingers, and place upright, rounded side out, around side of bowl.

Basic Fruit Juice Whip

You asked for it—and Knox test kitchens did it—way back in the 1960's. A low-calorie but really great-tasting dessert.

1 envelope Knox Unflavored Gelatine
2 Tbs. sugar
1 cup water or fruit juice, heated to boiling*
1 cup cold fruit juice

In large bowl, mix Unflavored Gelatine with sugar; add boiling water or fruit juice and stir until Gelatine is completely dissolved. Stir in cold juice. Chill, stirring occasionally, until mixture is consistency of unbeaten egg whites. With electric mixer, beat at high speed until mixture triples in volume; about 10 minutes. Turn into dessert dishes or large bowl and chill until set. Makes about 8 servings.

Variations: Try any of the following fruit juices—orange, pineapple (do not use fresh or frozen), grape juice, apricot or peach nectar or cranberry juice cocktail.

* NOTE: Use all juices for fruitier flavor. If *less* sweetness is desired, reduce sugar.

Grasshopper Dessert

A variation of a favorite, lighter than grasshopper pie, it's been a "collectible recipe" since Jell-O printed it on their Lime Jell-O box a decade ago.

    2 3-oz. packages or 1 6-oz. package Jell-O Lime
      Gelatin
1½ cups cold water
  ¼ cup sugar
    2 cups boiling water
    2 Tbs. green creme de menthe liqueur
    1 envelope Dream Whip Whipped Topping mix

Dissolve gelatin and sugar in boiling water. Add cold water and liqueur. Pour 1 cup into a bowl and chill slightly, until slightly thickened. Pour remaining gelatin mixture into a 9-inch square pan. Chill until firm—at least 3 hours. Cut into ½-inch squares.

  Meanwhile, prepare whipped topping mix as directed on package. Blend into slightly thickened gelatin. Pour into a 3-cup bowl. Chill until firm—about 3 hours. Unmold the creamy gelatin in the center of a shallow serving bowl. Arrange gelatin cubes around the mold. Garnish with chocolate curls, if desired. Makes about 5 cups or 8–10 servings.

Topaz Parfait

Beautiful to look at and absolutely divine to eat. A perfect "make ahead" dessert for your next dinner party. The recipe is from the Lemon Jell-O box. If you meant to save it but didn't, fret not, here it is.

  1 cup strong coffee
  1 3-oz. package Jell-O Lemon Gelatin
  ⅓ cup sugar

½ cup cold water*
¼ cup brandy or dark rum*
1 envelope Dream Whip Whipped Topping mix
2 Tbs. brown sugar
1 Tbs. brandy or dark rum**

Bring coffee to a boil. Add gelatin and sugar and stir until dissolved. Add cold water and ¼ cup brandy. Pour into an 8-inch square pan. Chill until firm—about 4 hours. Cut into cubes. Prepare whipped topping as directed adding brown sugar and 1 Tbs. brandy. Layer coffee cubes and topping in parfait glasses or top cubes in sherbet glasses with topping. Makes 4 servings.

Note: Recipe may be doubled.

* Or increase cold water to ¾ cup and add 1 tsp. brandy extract.
** Or use ½ tsp. brandy extract.

Patriotic Mold

It's the Fourth of July! Plan a porch supper of cold fried chicken, corn on the cob, sliced tomatoes and onions; wind up with this red, white and blue spectacular! As much fun as fireworks, and a dream to taste.

Red Layer:

1 3-oz. package Jell-O Strawberry Gelatin
1⅓ cups boiling water
1 10-oz. package Birds-Eye Quick-Thaw
   Strawberries

White Layer:

1 3-oz. package Jell-O Lemon Gelatin
1 cup boiling water
1 pint vanilla ice cream, slightly softened

Blue Layer:

1 package 3-oz. Jell-O—Lemon, Black Cherry,
   Concord Grape or Black Raspberry—Gelatin
¼ cup sugar
1 cup boiling water
½ cup cold water
1½ cups fresh, frozen or drained canned
   blueberries, mashed.

Dissolve strawberry gelatin in 1⅓ cups boiling water. Add frozen strawberries. Stir gently until fruit thaws and separates. Chill until thickened. Pour into an 8-cup mold (star-shaped, if desired), a 9-cup Bundt pan, or straight-sided saucepan. Chill until set, but not firm.

Dissolve 1 package lemon gelatin in 1 cup boiling water. Blend in ice cream, beating until smooth. Chill until thickened. Spoon over strawberry mixture in mold. Chill until set, but not firm.

Dissolve remaining package of gelatin and the sugar in 1 cup boiling water. Add ½ cup cold water; chill until thickened. Stir in blueberries and spoon over lemon ice cream mixture in mold. Chill until firm, or overnight. Unmold. Makes about 8 cups or 12–14 servings.

Frozen Pumpkin Dessert Squares

This "new" way to serve pumpkin made its appearence back in 1960 when the recipe was first printed on Libby's solid pack pumpkin can. It's as American as pumpkin pie and just as delicious.

1½ cups graham cracker crumbs
¼ cup sugar
¼ cup butter or margarine, melted

1 16-oz. can Libby's Solid Pack Pumpkin
½ cup brown sugar
½ tsp. salt
1 tsp. ground cinnamon
¼ tsp. ground ginger
⅛ tsp. ground cloves
1 quart vanilla ice cream, softened
    Whipped cream and toasted coconut
    (optional)

Mix crumbs with sugar and butter. Press into bottom of
9-inch square pan. Combine pumpkin with brown sugar,
salt and spices. Fold in ice cream. Pour into crumb-lined
pan. Cover; freeze until firm. Take out of freezer about 20
minutes before serving. Cut into squares; top each
square with whipped cream and toasted coconut. Yields
9 3-inch squares.

Ice Cream Sandwiches

**A Sunday best dessert, easy to do and prepared ahead of
time. Kellogg's® Rice Krispies cereal featured the ice cream
treat in national advertising two summers ago, and put it on
their cereal box too.**

½ cup corn syrup
½ cup peanut butter
4 cups Kellogg's® Rice Krispies cereal
1 pint ice cream, cut into 6 slices

In medium size mixing bowl, stir together corn syrup and
peanut butter. Add Kellogg's® Rice Krispies cereal. Stir
until well coated. Press mixture evenly in buttered
13 × 9 × 2-inch pan. Place in freezer or coldest part of
refrigerator until firm. Cut cereal mixture into twelve

3-inch squares. Sandwich each slice of ice cream between 2 squares. Freeze until firm. Cut each large
sandwich in half and wrap individually in foil. Store in
freezer until needed. Makes 12 sandwiches.

PET® EVAPORATED MILK ICE CREAMS

**I just went wild when I sampled these luxurious Ice Creams.
So instead of stingily giving you just one I have included
them all.**

Fudge Marlow

1 13-oz. can Pet®
   Evaporated Milk, divided
   usage
⅔ cup sugar
⅓ cup cocoa

Few grains salt
½ cup water
16 large marshmallows
2 tsps. vanilla

Freeze 1 cup evaporated milk in small mixing bowl until
ice crystals form along edges. Stir together sugar, cocoa
and salt in small saucepan. Add ⅔ cup evaporated milk
and water. Cook and stir over low heat until smooth. Add
marshmallows and cook until half melted. Remove from
heat. Stir until completely melted. Stir in vanilla. Pour
into medium bowl. Refrigerate until well chilled. Beat icy
evaporated milk until stiff. Fold into chilled cocoa mixture. Pour into 2½ quart bowl. Freeze until firm. Makes
about 2 quarts.

Coffee Pecan Ice Cream

2 eggs
1⅓ cups sugar
2 13-oz. cans Pet®
   Evaporated Milk
1 cup whole milk

1 Tbs. vanilla
2 Tbs. instant coffee
¼ cup boiling water
1 cup chopped pecans

Beat eggs and sugar in large mixing bowl until well blended. Stir in evaporated milk, milk and vanilla. Dissolve coffee in boiling water. Add to milk mixture. Refrigerate until well chilled. Pour into ice cream freezer container. Churn and freeze according to manufacturer's directions. When ice cream is finished, stir in pecans.

Mint Chip Ice Cream

3 eggs
1½ cups sugar
2 13-oz. cans Pet®
   Evaporated Milk

¾ tsp. peppermint extract
⅛ tsp. green food coloring
1½ cups (6 oz.) grated milk
   chocolate

Beat eggs and sugar in large mixing bowl until well blended. Stir in evaporated milk, peppermint extract and food coloring. Gently stir in grated chocolate. Refrigerate until well chilled. Pour into ice cream freezer container. Churn and freeze according to manufacturer's directions. Makes about 2 quarts.

Cinnamon Chocolate Ice Cream

3 13-oz. cans Pet®
   Evaporated Milk,
   divided usage
2½ 1-oz. squares
   unsweetened chocolate

2 eggs
1 cup sugar
½ tsp. cinnamon
¼ tsp. nutmeg

Combine 1 can (1⅔ cups) evaporated milk and chocolate in small saucepan. Cook over medium heat, stirring frequently, until chocolate melts and mixture is smooth. Meanwhile beat eggs, sugar, cinnamon and nutmeg in large mixing bowl until well blended. Stir in hot chocolate mixture. Stir in remaining 2 cans (3⅓ cups) evaporated milk. Refrigerate until well chilled. Pour into ice cream freezer container. Churn and freeze according to manufacturer's directions. Makes 2 quarts.

Peanut Butter Chocolate Ice Cream

2 13-oz. cans Pet® Evaporated Milk, divided
   usage
2 squares (2 oz.) unsweetened chocolate
2 eggs
¾ cup sugar
4–6 Tbs. chunky peanut butter

Combine 1 cup evaporated milk and chocolate in small saucepan. Cook over medium heat, stirring frequently, until chocolate melts and mixture is smooth. Meanwhile beat eggs and sugar in large mixing bowl until well blended. Beat in peanut butter until smooth. Stir in hot chocolate mixture. Stir in remaining 2⅓ cups evaporated milk. Refrigerate until well chilled. Pour into ice cream freezer container. Churn and freeze according to manufacturer's directions. Makes about 2 quarts.

10.
Cookies
and
Candies

For a while there I began to think nobody made cookies anymore—or homemade candy, for that matter. Everyone seemed to be so "into gourmet" that the humble cookie and the plate of homemade fudge became somewhat out of fashion. Well, the cookie is back; and who can wonder why after they taste cookies like our California Gold Bars or deep, dark, chewy Chocolate Brownies? As for candy, a lot of people are discovering that a plate of homemade candies offered with small cups of hot strong coffee makes the perfect finale to the most elegant dinner party.

Nothing could be easier or more satisfying than to whip up a few dozen cookies or a platter of candy. Even busier-than-ever cooks can find the few moments it takes with any of the recipes included here. As for saving money as well as time, homemade beats "store bought" by a country mile.

Once again I assure you that each recipe here is a proven success, easy, quick and dependable time after time—tested over and over again in the kitchens of our most famous food companies. All you need to worry about is making enough; the cookies and candies included here have a way of vanishing—fast!

California Gold Bars

Oh my, these are good! A top-request recipe. If you bought a 2-pound box of Domino® Granulated Sugar about 5 years ago, you may already have it on file.

1½ cups (11-oz. package) dried apricots
4 eggs
2 cups Domino® Granulated Sugar
½ tsp. salt
2 tsps. grated orange rind

2 cups sifted all-purpose flour
2 tsps. double-acting baking powder
½ tsp. nutmeg
1 cup chopped pecans or walnuts
Domino® Confectioners' 10-X Powdered Sugar

Soak apricots in water until soft. Drain well; cut into small pieces. Beat eggs well in large bowl. Gradually beat sugar and salt into eggs until light and foamy. Add orange rind. Sift together flour, baking powder and nutmeg; gradually blend into egg mixture. Add apricots and nuts; mix briefly. Spread batter into 2 greased 9-inch square pans. Bake in moderate oven, 350°F., 30–35 minutes or until done. When partially cool, cut 1½ × 3-inch bars and roll in confectioners' sugar. Remove to cooling rack. If necessary to store bars, place in air-tight container with waxed paper between layers; roll again in confectioners' sugar before serving. Yields 54 bars.

Lemony Bars

I just love this recipe; it's super easy, inexpensive and so delicious. Makes super bars to serve as cookies, but I also like to cut it into squares and serve with a scoop of vanilla ice cream or a fluff of whipped cream as a heavenly dessert. The cooks at the Checkerboard Kitchens dreamed it up for their Rice Chex® Cereal box about six years ago.

Base	**Topping**

Base
- 1 cup sifted all-purpose flour
- ¾ cup sugar
- ½ tsp. baking powder
- ¼ tsp. salt
- 2 cups Rice Chex® cereal crushed to ½ cup
- ½ cup butter or margarine

Topping
- 2 eggs, beaten
- ¾ cup sugar
- 2 Tbs. all-purpose flour
- ¼ tsp. baking powder
- 4 tsps. lemon juice
- 1 tsp. grated lemon peel

Preheat oven to 350°F. Grease 9-inch square baking pan. To prepare *base*, sift together flour, sugar, baking powder and salt. Stir in Rice Chex crumbs. Cut in butter until very fine crumbs. Press mixture firmly into pan. Bake 12 minutes.

Meanwhile, prepare *topping*. Combine all ingredients. Mix until well blended. Pour over hot base. Return to oven for additional 15–20 minutes or until top is set but not browned. Cool. Sprinkle with confectioners' sugar. Cut into bars. Makes 24 (2¼ × 1½-inch) bars.

Almond Blondies

Here's another recipe for cookie bars that can be cut into squares and can double as a very special dessert. It's from the Blue-Diamond® Almond can and I think you will love it.

- ⅓ cup shortening
- 1 cup granulated sugar
- 2 eggs
- 2 tsps. vanilla extract
- 1⅓ cups all-purpose flour (do not sift)
- 1 cup flaked coconut
- 2 tsps. baking powder
- ½ tsp. salt
- Topping (below)

Cream shortening with granulated sugar; beat in eggs and vanilla. Sprinkle flour, coconut, baking powder and salt over creamed mixture; beat well. Spread over bottom of 9-inch square baking pan. Spoon Topping over evenly. Bake in 350°F. oven 40 to 50 minutes or until a light touch in center leaves no impression. Cut into 1½-inch rectangles. Makes about 3 dozen.

Topping

½ cup Blue-Diamond® Whole Blanched
   Almonds, toasted
½ cup packed brown sugar
1 Tbs. all-purpose flour
1 egg
¼ cup heavy cream

Coarsely chop almonds. Combine with brown sugar and flour. Stir in egg and cream.

Crunchy Chews

Rich, moist, chewy and delicious; quick and easy to prepare. You'll love these bar cookies from the Skippy Peanut Butter kitchens.

¾ cup sugar
¾ cup Karo Dark Corn Syrup
¾ cup Skippy Super Chunk Peanut Butter
4½ cups corn flakes, crisp rice cereal or round
   oat cereal
¾ cup peanuts or broken mixed nuts (optional)

Grease 13 × 9 × 2-inch baking pan. In saucepan mix together sugar and corn syrup. Bring to boil, stirring constantly, over medium heat. Boil 1 minute. Mix in peanut butter. Turn into prepared pan. Stir in corn flakes and nuts. Press together firmly. Cool. Cut into squares. Makes 4½ dozen (1½-inch) squares.

Fudgy Brownies

Here it is, just what you asked for, that *other* brownie recipe, the chewy, fudgy dark chocolate kind. From Baker's Chocolate.

4 squares Baker's Unsweetened Chocolate
½ cup butter or margarine
2 cups sugar
4 eggs, beaten
1 cup sifted flour
1 tsp. vanilla
1 cup coarsely chopped walnuts

Melt chocolate and butter together over hot water. Cool slightly. Gradually add sugar to eggs, beating thoroughly after each addition. Blend in chocolate mixture. Stir in flour. Then add vanilla and nuts. Spread in greased 9-inch square pan. Bake in slow oven (325°F.) about 40 minutes. Cool in pan. Cut into squares. Makes about 2 dozen brownies.

Chocolate Peppermint Brownies: Prepare Fudgy Brownies, arranging 15–20 chocolate peppermint patties over top of hot brownies; return to oven about 3 minutes to soften patties. Then spread to cover entire top of the brownies. Cool and cut.

Nut-Topped Brownies: Prepare Fudgy Brownies, omitting walnuts from batter. Pour batter into pan and sprinkle with ½ cup coarsely chopped walnuts, pecans or peanuts. Bake. If desired, melt 1 square Baker's Unsweetened or Semi-Sweet Chocolate with 1 tsp. butter; blend, and dribble over top of baked brownies.

Honey Brownies (formerly Honeybear Brownies)

Was the first baking you ever did a pan of Honeybear Brownies? Mine was. The recipe was from the label of a can of Hershey's Cocoa and everyone said they were the "best ever." I still make them and you know what? They still say just that.

⅓ cup butter or margarine	½ cup unsifted all-purpose
¾ cup sugar	flour
⅓ cup honey	⅓ cup Hershey's Cocoa
2 tsps. vanilla	½ tsp. salt
2 eggs	1 cup chopped nuts

Grease one 9-inch pan. Cream butter and sugar in small mixer bowl; blend in honey and vanilla. Add eggs, one at a time, beating well after each addition. Combine flour, cocoa and salt; gradually add to creamed mixture. Stir in nuts. Pour into pan. Bake at 350°F. for 25–30 minutes or until brownies begin to pull away from edge of pan. Cool in pan. Makes 16 brownies.

Peanut Butter Brownies

Two American favorites; chocolate and peanut butter combine in these moist, rich and delicious brownies. The recipe was perfected by the good cooks at Reese's.

½ cup butter or margarine, softened
   Peanut Butter Brownie Frosting (below)
1 cup sugar
1 tsp. vanilla
2 eggs
1¼ cups unsifted all-purpose flour
⅛ tsp. baking soda
¾ cup Hershey's Chocolate Syrup
1 cup Reese's Peanut Butter Chips

Cream butter or margarine, sugar and vanilla. Add eggs; beat well. Combine flour and baking soda; add alternately with chocolate syrup to creamed mixture. Stir in peanut butter chips. Pour batter into greased 13 × 9 × 2-inch pan; bake at 350°F. for 30–35 minutes. Cool; frost with Peanut Butter Brownie Frosting. Makes 24 brownies.

Peanut Butter Brownie Frosting: Combine ⅓ cup sugar, ¼ cup evaporated milk and 2 Tbs. butter in a small saucepan. Stir over medium heat until mixture comes to full boil; remove from heat. Quickly stir in 1 cup Reese's Peanut Butter Chips until melted; add 1 tsp. vanilla. Beat to spreading consistency; frost brownies. Cut into 24 brownies.

Queen's Lace Cookies

The nuns at the convent near our house in Louisiana used to make cookies like these; I always thought they were impossibly difficult until I discovered the recipe in the Parkay Margarine cookbook. If you want to make an impression at your next party, these are for you.

¼ cup Squeeze Parkay Margarine	½ cup flour
¼ cup granulated sugar	½ tsp. grated lemon rind
2 Tbs. dark corn syrup	¼ tsp. ginger
1 tsp. brandy	Brandied Whipped Cream (below)

Heat margarine, granulated sugar and corn syrup over low heat in heavy skillet or saucepan, stirring until sugar is dissolved. Remove from heat; beat in brandy and combined flour, lemon rind and ginger. Drop level teaspoonfuls of batter, 3 inches apart, onto greased cookie sheet. Bake at 350°F., 8–10 minutes or until deep golden brown. Remove from oven; wait 10–15 seconds for cookies to set. Remove cookies one at a time; turn smooth-side up and wrap around handle of a wooden spoon spread with margarine. Slip cookie off; repeat with remaining cookies, working quickly. If cookies become too firm to roll, return to oven for 1–2 minutes to soften. When ready to serve, fill cookies with Brandied Whipped Cream.

Brandied Whipped Cream

1 cup heavy cream	1 Tbs. brandy
2 Tbs. confectioners' sugar	

Whip cream until slightly thickened; gradually add sugar and brandy, beating until stiff peaks form. Makes enough to fill approximately 1½ dozen cookies.

Melting Moments

The Argo Company tells me there have been dozens of variations on this recipe since it first appeared on their packaging some thirty years ago, but this was the original and the texture and flavor can't be improved. You can add chopped nuts, coconut or candied fruit or top each cookie with a whole pe-

can, almond, or candied cherry—but then I don't have to tell you, do I?

1 cup unsifted flour
½ cup Argo or Kingsford's Corn Starch
½ cup confectioners' sugar
¾ cup Nucoa or Mazola Margarine

In medium bowl stir flour, cornstarch and confectioners' sugar. In large bowl with mixer at medium speed beat margarine until smooth. Add flour mixture and beat until combined. Refrigerate 1 hour. Shape into 1-inch balls. Place about 1½ inches apart on ungreased cookie sheet; flatten with lightly floured fork. Bake in 300°F. oven 20 minutes or until edges are lightly browned. Makes about 3 dozen cookies.

Chinese Almond Cookies

This recipe was developed because of popular demand. When Oriental cooking started to become popular in this country about ten years ago, requests came in to the Almond Growers Exchange so hot and heavy that a recipe had to be perfected. This one is perfection indeed.

½ cup Blue-Diamond® Whole Natural Almonds
1 cup sifted all-purpose flour
½ tsp. baking powder
¼ tsp. salt
½ cup butter or margarine
⅓ cup granulated sugar
½ tsp. almond extract
1 Tbs. gin, vodka or water

Reserve 36 whole almonds; finely chop or grind remainder. Sift flour with baking powder and salt. Thoroughly cream butter and sugar. Stir in all remaining ingredients except whole almonds. Form dough into 36 balls. Place on greased cookie sheets. Press a whole almond in center of each ball. Bake in 350°F. oven for 20 minutes or until lightly browned. Makes about 3 dozen.

Old-Fashioned Molasses Cookies

If there are children in your house, these cookies belong in a cookie jar on a low shelf in your kitchen. Made with Elam's extra-nutritional flours.

1 cup Elam's Stone Ground 100% Whole Wheat
  Flour
¾ cup Elam's Unbleached White Flour with
  Wheat Germ
½ tsp. salt
½ tsp. baking soda
½ tsp. cinnamon
½ cup soft shortening or butter
¾ cup (packed) brown sugar
 1 egg
¼ cup molasses

Combine and mix first 5 ingredients in bowl; reserve. Beat shortening or butter until creamy. Add brown sugar gradually; beat well after each addition. Add egg and molasses; beat until smooth. Blend in dry ingredients; mix well. Chill dough 1–2 hours. Shape dough into balls using a level Tbs. of dough for each. Place balls 2 inches apart on ungreased baking sheets. Bake in slow oven (325°F.) until done, 15– 18 minutes. Transfer to wire racks to cool. Yields about 3½ dozen cookies, 2½ inches in diameter.

Oatmeal Drop Cookies

Old friends are best, and what better and older friends does a child of any age have than an oatmeal cookie and a glass of cold milk. These are the real thing from Elam's. Great tasting and nutritional, too.

2 cups Elam's Stone Ground 100% Whole Wheat Flour
1 tsp. salt
1 tsp. baking soda
1 tsp. cinnamon
2 cups Elam's Steel Cut Oatmeal
1 cup soft shortening
½ cup (packed) brown sugar

1 egg
2 tsps. vanilla
½ cup light corn syrup
⅓ cup milk
1 cup seedless raisins
1 cup chopped pecans or walnuts

Combine and mix whole wheat flour, salt, soda and cinnamon. Stir in oatmeal; reserve. Beat shortening and sugar together until creamy. Beat in egg and vanilla. Add dry ingredients alternately with corn syrup and milk, blending well after each addition. Stir in raisins and nuts. Drop rounded tablespoonfuls of dough onto ungreased baking sheets. Bake in moderate oven (350°F.) until done and brown, 12– 14 minutes. Yields about 5½ dozen cookies, about 2½ inches in diameter.

Easy Baking 'n' Making Cookies

A favorite treat for children, young men and women, older ladies and gentlemen and just about everyone in between. Has been since it was first printed on the 5-pound bag of Domino® Granulated Sugar.

1 cup butter or margarine
½ cup peanut butter
1 cup Domino® Granulated Sugar
½ cup firmly packed Domino® Light Brown Sugar
1 egg
⅓ cup pancake syrup
1 tsp. vanilla
1½ cups sifted all-purpose flour
2 tsps. baking powder
Dash of salt
1½ cups old-fashioned or quick-rolled oats
1 cup coconut

Cream butter, peanut butter and sugars; beat in egg, syrup and vanilla. Sift together flour, baking powder and salt; beat into creamed mixture until blended; stir in oats and coconut. Drop by teaspoonfuls onto greased cookie sheets. Bake in moderate oven, 350°F., 12–15 minutes. Yields 6 dozen cookies.

Bourbon Balls

Christmas wouldn't be Christmas to us Southerners without Bourbon for eggnog, pecans for turkey stuffing, and both for cookies like these. One of the most popular recipes from the Karo Corn Syrup label.

3½ cups vanilla wafer crumbs (about 12 oz.)
1½ cup confectioners' sugar, divided
1 cup finely chopped pecans
¼ cup unsweetened cocoa
⅓ cup bourbon
⅓ cup Karo Light Corn Syrup

In large bowl stir together crumbs, 1 cup of the confectioners' sugar, pecans and cocoa. Stir in bourbon and corn syrup until well blended. Shape into 1-inch balls. Roll in remaining confectioners' sugar. Store in tightly covered container. Makes about 4½ dozen.

Fudge

Now who doesn't love creamy smooth fudge? But therein lies the problem—gritty fudge or fudge that refuses to harden. To avoid such unhappiness, make your next batch of fudge from this famous Hershey's recipe.

⅔ cup Hershey's Cocoa
3 cups sugar
⅛ tsp. salt
1½ cups milk
¼ cup butter or margarine
1 tsp. vanilla

Lightly grease 8- or 9-inch square pan. Thoroughly combine dry ingredients in a heavy 4-quart saucepan; stir in milk. Bring to a "bubbly" boil on medium heat, stirring constantly. Boil without stirring to 234°F. (soft-ball stage). (Bulb of candy thermometer should not rest on bottom of saucepan.) Remove from heat; add butter and vanilla. Do not stir. Cool at room temperature to 110°F. (pan is barely warm to touch). Beat with wooden spoon until fudge thickens and loses its gloss. Quickly spread in pan.

Marshmallow-Nut Variation: Increase Hershey's Cocoa to ¾ cup. Cook fudge as above. Add 1 cup marshmallow creme with butter and vanilla. Do not stir. Cool to 110°F. Beat 10 minutes; stir in 1 cup broken nuts and pour into pan. (Fudge will not set until it is poured into pan.)

Chocolate "Philly" Fudge

When "Philly" Fudge was first demonstrated on television in 1951, over a million viewers requested the recipe.

4 cups sifted confectioners'
sugar
1 8-oz. package
Philadelphia Brand
Cream Cheese
4 1-oz. squares
unsweetened chocolate,
melted

1 tsp. vanilla
Dash of salt
½ cup chopped nuts

Gradually add sugar to softened cream cheese, mixing until well blended. Stir in remaining ingredients. Spread in greased 8-inch square pan. Chill several hours or overnight. Makes 1¾ pounds.

Easy Peanut Butter Fudge

A favorite in the Skippy recipe files. If you want a peanut butter candy both extra easy and extra good, this is it.

1 15-oz. can sweetened condensed milk
½ cup Skippy Creamy or Super Chunk Peanut
Butter
½ cup Karo Dark Corn Syrup
½ tsp. salt
1 lb. confectioners' sugar

Grease 9 × 9 × 2-inch baking pan. In 2-quart saucepan stir together condensed milk, peanut butter, corn syrup and salt. Cook over low heat, stirring frequently, 15 minutes or until thick. Gradually add confectioners' sugar, stirring until blended. (If mixture becomes too stiff, knead with hands.) Press into prepared pan. Refrigerate several hours or until firm. Cut into 1-inch squares. Store in tightly covered container in refrigerator. Makes 2½ pounds.

Angel Divinity

Perhaps you never made Divinity candy because you were told it was tricky. Not with this recipe; it's been tested at the Baker Coconut kitchens and by thousands of pleased and proud cooks.

½ cup light corn syrup
2½ cups sugar
¼ tsp. salt
½ cup water
2 egg whites, stiffly beaten
1½ tsps. vanilla
　Few drops peppermint flavoring (optional)

½ cup chopped nuts
1 cup Baker's Angel Flake, Premium Shred, Southern Style, or Cookie Coconut

Combine corn syrup, sugar, salt and water in sauce-pan. Cook and stir over medium heat, until sugar is dissolved. Continue cooking, without stirring, until a small amount of syrup forms a hard ball in cold water—or to a temperature of 262°F. Then pour syrup slowly over beaten egg whites, beating constantly. Beat until mixture begins to dull and hold its shape. Add flavorings and nuts. Drop from tip of tsp. into coconut on wax paper; roll to shape candy into a ball and to coat with coconut. Decorate with maraschino cherries, if desired. Makes about 7 dozen candies.

OLD-FASHIONED CANDY

- -

This is the all-time top-request recipe at holiday time from Domino® Granulated Sugar test kitchens.

(Start with this syrup and use in the following recipes)

Syrup

6 cups Domino® Granulated Sugar
3 cups water
¾ tsp. cream of tartar

Cook these ingredients quickly without stirring to 290°F.

Candied Apples or Pears

Add a few drops of red food coloring. Place pan in hot water to keep syrup from hardening. Begin dipping skewered apples or pears at once. Cool on greased surface. Makes enough to coat 9 medium apples or pears.

Old-Fashioned Rock Candy

Substitute fruit juice for liquid, or add flavored extract and desired food coloring. Pour quickly into greased square pan. Chill until firm. Turn out of pan; crack into desired pieces. Yields 2 pounds.

Party Shapes

Pour rock candy mixture into individually shaped molds, ¼ inch thick. Chill. Makes approximately 1 dozen.

Index

Bean(s) (*cont.*):
  baked with wieners, 16
  and chili beef, 10
  green (*see* Green beans)
  Hawaiian, 63
  salad Italian, 82
Beef barbecue sauce, 71
Beef Burgundy with rice, 8
Beef, chili and beans, 10
Beer batter for fish or shrimp,
  25
Beets in a mustard ring, 90
Biscuits, baking powder, 132
Biscuits, quick mix, 134
Black Forest cake, 153
Blue cheese dressing, 94
Blueberry muffins, 140
Boatman's stew, 26
Boston burgers, 115
Boston cream pie, 169
Bourbon balls, 220
Brandy Alexander pie, 179
Breads, 125–146
  caramel crescent swirl,
    144
  corn, 135
  date and nut, 143
  gingerbread, 145
  quick mix, 133
  quick nut, 142
  Sally Lunn, 131
  tea loaf, 141
  whole wheat, 128
  (*See also* Muffins, Rolls)
Broccoli, elegant puffed, 59

Brown Betty, raisin, 194
Brownies, 213–214
Brunch-wich, original, 119
Brunch-wich, pizza, 119
Burgers, 114–117
  Balboa party, 114
  Boston, 114
  piñata, 115
  rancheros, 114
  Scotch, 117
Burgundy steak sauce à la
    Worcester, 68

Cake fillings, 154–156, 190
Cakes, 147–168
  apple, fresh, 165
  apple spice coffee, 142
  Black Forest, 153
  chocolate sour cream, 155
  chocolate, sweet, 156
  chocolate town special, 158
  cheesecake, 152
  coconut prize, 161
  fruit gâteau, 168
  fudge, 158
  graham cracker, 162
  orange-raisin whole wheat,
    167
  peanut butter picnic, 163
  raisin nut, 166
  shortcake supreme, 190
  spice, 151
  tea ring, Swedish, 138
  Tennessee jam, 164

Fish (*cont.*):
  Imperial Baltimore, 30
  pie, savory, 42
  salmon dill mousse, 90
  salmon quiche, 41
  sole en croute, 32
  stew, boatman's, 26
  teriyaki fillets, 33
  (See *also* Shrimp; Tuna)
Flounder (see Fish)
Fondue, chocolate, 193
Franks, barbecued cocktail,
    100
  sweet and sour, 106
Franks and spaghetti, 37
Freckled-face 'taters, 53
French dressings, 92, 94
French fries, 50
Frostings:
  brandied whipped cream,
    216
  brown sugar, 164
  chocolate cream topping,
    178
  chocolate glazes, 161, 170
  chocolate sour cream, 156
  coconut, golden, 159
  coconut-pecan, 157
  honey-nut, 168
  honey spread, 139
  peanut butter, 163
  peanut butter brownie, 314
  vanilla drizzle, 139
  whipped cream, 155
Fruit gâteau, 168

Fruit juice whip, 198
Fruit salad, 91
Fruit tarts, 181
Fruit yogurt dressing, 93
Fudge, 221–222
Fudge cake, 158
Fudge Marlow, 203
Fudgy casserole à la mode,
    191

Gingerbread, 145
Goulash, veal, 11
Graham cracker cake, 162
Grasshopper dessert, 199
Green beans polonaise, 57
Green beans, sour creamed,
    56
Green goddess dressing, 95

Hot dogs (see Franks)
Halibut (see Fish)
Ham corn bread pie, 45
Ham, golden glaze, 13
Ham, grilled salad and
    cheese sandwich, 120
Ham tidbits Oriental, 100
Hamburgers (see Burgers)
Hash, rodeo, 10
Hens, Cornish, 23
Honey brownies, 214
Honey-nut topping, 168
Honey spread, 139
Horseradish dip, 101
Horseradish sauce, 74

Iberia French dressing, 92

Raisin brown Betty, 194
Raisin nut cake, 166
Raisin nut pie, 174
Reuben sandwiches, open-
  faced, 121
Ribs, barbecued Korean-
  style, 106
Rice, Pilaf, 55
Rice, Spanish, 54
Rice, wild, chicken supreme,
  21
Roast, New England boiled
  dinner, 7
Roast, Western pot, 4
Rock candy, 225
Rodeo hash, 100
Roll(s):
  coconut sponge, 136
  dinner, frozen, 130
  sixty-minute, 129
  two-hour nut, 136

Salads, 77–92
  Acapulco, 85
  avocado and mushroom, 86
  bean, Italian, 82
  beets in a mustard ring, 90
  chutney ham, 80
  cole slaw, 84
  corn 'n' cucumbers, 84
  egg, 123
  ensalada verde, 86
  fruit, 91
  garden fresh, 88
  macaroni, all-American, 83

Salads (cont.):
  macaroni, supper, 80
  salmon dill mousse, 90
  salmon sesame boats, 81
  spring sandwich, 122
  summer, with sour cream
    dressing, 89
  tuna, crisp and crunchy, 81
  vegetable, sliced Califor-
    nia, 83
  Waldorf à la Russe, 87
Salisbury steak, 7
Sally Lunn, 131
Salmon (see Fish)
Sandwiches, 111– 124
  brunch-wich, original, 119
    pizza, 119
  club, California, 120
  Coney Islands, 121
  egg salad, 123
  ham salad 'n' cheese,
    grilled, 120
  peanut butter 'n' bacon, 124
  Reubens, open-faced, 121
  sausage en croute, 122
  sausage and pepper filled
    deli rolls, 118
  spring salad, 122
  tuna bunwiches, 116
  (See also Burgers)
Sauces, 65– 76
  apple and raisin for ham,
    71
  barbecue for hot dogs, 72
  barbecue, Texas, 73

About the Author

Ceil Dyer is the author of fifteen cookbooks, the most recent of which are *Wok Cookery* and *The Carter Family Favorites Cookbook*, in addition to McGraw-Hill's *Best Recipes from the Backs of Boxes, Bottles, Cans and Jars*, in both hardcover and paperback, which is a selection of the Cookbook Guild. Ms. Dyer has had five other cookbooks selected by the Guild.